The Education of Black Folk

Date Due

BRODART, CO.   Cat. No. 23-233-003   Printed in U.S.A.

The Education of Black Folk

The Afro-American Struggle for Knowledge in White America

ALLEN B. BALLARD

AN AUTHORS GUILD BACKINPRINT.COM EDITION

The Education of Black Folk
The Afro-American Struggle for Knowledge in White America

AN AUTHORS GUILD BACKINPRINT.COM EDITION
Published by iUniverse, Inc.

For information address:
iUniverse, Inc.
2021 Pine Lake Road, Suite 100
Lincoln, NE 68512
www.iuniverse.com

Originally published by Harper & Row

First HARPER COLOPHON edition 1974.

Designed by C. Linda Dingler

ISBN: 0-595-31766-9

Printed in the United States of America

Contents

Acknowledgments

I would like to thank Scott Anderson and Nancy Clare for assisting me in the research for this book. I would also like to thank especially Celia Urquhart for her total assistance in putting the manuscript together.

Leslie Berger, Addison Gayle, Henry Harris, Dean Harrison, Raymond Murphy, Mina Shaughnessy, Hugh Lane, T. McKinney, Les Jacobs, Timothy S. Healy and other friends read parts or all of the manuscript and made helpful criticisms. They, of course, are in no way responsible for the content or views expressed therein. Jeannette Hopkins, of Harper & Row, and her editorial assistant, Susan Hitchcock, gave helpful and skilled advice throughout the writing of the manuscript.

Finally, and most important, I want to express my thanks to the staff and students of the SEEK program at City College for demonstrating, through their dedication and persistence against sometimes almost insurmountable odds, that the elitist theory of education rests on the slimmest of reeds—the belief that some are endowed from birth with the ability to learn and that others, of a different skin color, are doomed forever to be separated from that knowledge necessary to survival in the modern world.

To
Alayna and John
and in loving memory of
Betty Rawls,
Alfred Conrad,
Lloyd Delaney,

without whose steadfast and unswerving
sense of mission thousands of black and
Puerto Rican students presently enrolled
in the City University would have been
rejected as "uneducable"

They were right when they sought to found a new educational system upon the University: where, forsooth, shall we ground knowledge save on the broadest and deepest knowledge? The roots of the tree, rather than the leaves, are the sources of its life; and from the dawn of history, from Academus to Cambridge, the culture of the University has been the broad foundation-stone on which is built the kindergarten's A B C.

—W. E. B. Du Bois, on post-Civil War Black educators, in *The Souls of Black Folks: Essays and Sketches*

The Educational Color Line in America

Few American students have ever taken the university seriously. And few universities have ever taken their students seriously. Neither had, until recently, paid serious attention to the status of Blacks in this society. For entry into college was an honor unto itself, a promissory note on the society's riches for any white student who dutifully completed his four years of study. Why should a university cater to students when the mere fact of finishing the institution promised a bounty denied to most of one's peers? And why should a student question an institution toward which societal and private pressures have been driving him since childhood? A college diploma was expected of well-to-do middle-class youth and demanded of those hoping to escape the lower classes. A depression, a postwar G.I. generation, and a decade of American normalcy in the 1950s assured peaceful coexistence between the university and its clientele. Alumni of the typical university might remember these decades in terms like this: "Old Professor Richards, a great guy, and sometimes he really made you think"; "Remember the time old John Jones got plowed in the Phi Delts and ran the hurdles sloshing in the milk punch?"; "Boy, were my folks proud when I graduated ninth in my class after working my way through school as a dishwasher."

The old grads who made these comments are probably now the vice-president of a major steel company, a law partner in a major Illinois firm, or a second secretary of an American embassy. But if one asked them about the Black students on their white campuses, probably one might recall, "We had a Negro captain of our Rose Bowl Team," and another, "They seemed to stick pretty close to themselves." They would not state the truth: "We never noticed them."

Just as students now question their college education, and colleges no longer take affectionate alumni and obedient students for granted, so more recent "old grads" will not have the luxury of ignoring Blacks. The "Guns of Willard Strait Hall" will resound in the minds of Cornell's 1969 class when they gather at reunions, if they do, to sing "Far Above Cayuga's Waters." City College's class of 1969 will not forget the fire-gutted interior of Aronow Auditorium, the heart of their student center. And UCLA's graduates will have to remember the pistol-fire that resulted in the death of two students in a dispute over a Black studies program. Nineteen sixty-nine was the year of the Black rebellion in American universities, and the consequences reduced some prominent college administrators to tears or emotional breakdowns, or led to their rapid exodus to foreign lands. College presidents, as they met in conventions and small foundation-funded discussion groups, asked each other: "Where did these students come from? Why can't they conform to the regular college order? Why are these young Blacks ungrateful when they were admitted with lower grades than those of regular students? What measures can we take to return to a normal state of affairs?"

The "normal state of affairs" characterized both the American university and most of its products in the past, and both reflected and reinforced the basic caste nature of the society at large. Upheavals on the campus tested that system and the country's willingness to remedy the racial injustice endemic to the system. The university's self-defined role of standing above societal and political conflict had been shown up as false. The one institution whose sanction is necessary to all those who would enter into the middle and upper middle classes had begun efforts to recruit ghetto youth. This encounter of Blacks and the academy had the explosive possibilities of water added to hydrochloric acid. Although the American university is the most truly conservative of all the society's institutions, the keeper of the culture, at the same time it must and does give the appearance of tolerating and encouraging dissenting views. Moreover, the American college regards itself as liberal on race. The prevailing assumption on most campuses is that racial prejudice is nonexistent in the academic world. All colleges, however, manifest white superiority; the new Black recruit sees these evidences of racism and responds with wrath. The combination of the tolerance of dissent and the unwillingness to admit bias produces the widespread vacillating conduct of college administrators and faculties when faced with Black campus insurrection. The university is both American and the American conscience and is therefore both causative of Black student unrest and capable of indecisive Hamlet-like behavior in response to the uproar. On the white campus, liberalism is impaled upon itself.

Black student disruption of the campus status quo is the inevitable consequence of the historical relationship of Blacks to higher education. Neither the Black colleges of the South nor the white colleges of the North and South recognized the true nature of their task; neither attempted to ensure that Black collegians would receive the same education as any other youth. Black colleges in the South, with rare exceptions, have traditionally been compelled to educate their students under paternalistic guidelines which precluded creativity and imposed a narrow curriculum. Those like Du Bois, who advocated the establishment of an alternative course of study, were rudely cast out by Black presidents doing the bidding of their white boards of overseers. There is a remarkable consistency between proposals made by Du Bois fifty years ago and demands put forth by Black students today— the connecting link, the belief that the peculiar circumstances of the Afro-American's sojourn in this country mandate a special approach to the education of Black youth.

The university today, as yesterday, is scarcely capable of adapting itself to the special needs of Black students. Like all institutions and persons, the American college harbors contradictory elements within itself while presenting an integrated front to the outside world. The university is a federal structure that functions well when all of its keepers agree on common goals; it flounders and disintegrates when there is no consensus on goals, and the fragility of the academic structure and the latent disruptive power of its constituent parts become apparent. Careful attention must be paid to the roles, ideologies, and powers of faculties, administrators, and students and the potential power of alumni, for the university is a multipurpose institution whose constituents reflect innumerable societal and economic interests that have excluded Blacks for as long as they have existed. When Black students enter this delicately balanced conglomerate of interests with a sense of their own interests and their own accumulated grievances, disequilibrium is an inevitable consequence. Their mere presence demands change, and this, in turn, means a shifting and realignment of power distribution on the campus.

The experiences of Afro-Americans who attended white colleges long ago give an additional perspective to the present malaise of Black students in white institutions. This writer himself, along with another Black, had the misfortune to become the first of our race to enter Kenyon College. In retrospect, it is clear that —with some exceptions—our existence on that campus was defined not by us but by the constant necessity to be everything that negated the white man's concept of niggers. We were, in fact, forced to suppress our natural inner selves so as to conform to the mores of a campus dominated by upper-middle-class Americans. For eighteen hours a day, our manners, speech, style of walking were on trial before white America. Classes, particularly in the freshman and sophomore years, although sometimes intellectually rewarding, seemed frequently to us tests to prove to both teachers and students that Jefferson's views on the Black mentality were incorrect. Social life revolved around the fraternities, from which we Blacks were automatically excluded. The cumulative toll, both psychically and academically, was heavy. Of eight students in the four years, five left for the military or large campuses close to urban centers. The only surcease from this eight-semester social ordeal for the three of us who remained came when the Black community in a nearby town provided us with Black warmth, food, and emotional support. We looked forward eagerly to weekends away from that alien campus.

We were not totally ignored by our white classmates. The liberal conscience could not tolerate that, and so we were duly elected to a variety of campus posts, from athletic captaincies to presidencies of various student bodies and membership in diverse honorary organizations. As we traveled on athletic trips and in search of female companionship around the small colleges of Pennsylvania, New York, and Ohio, we observed that most small white colleges had one or two Black students who were suffering bravely to prove the unprovable. The lone girl at one Ohio college broke into tears describing the desolate existence she led in that narrowly sectarian private institution in a town where no Black lived. It became evident that large colleges, with relatively numerous Black students and Black fraternal and sororal organizations, provided the social and psychological supports necessary to cope with hostile and indifferent institutions.

This theme of alienation among Blacks who had the singular chance to attend white institutions persisted in the pre-World War I and pre-World War II periods. Many seemed to feel themselves in four-year exile in a strange and alien white world which cut them off from their roots. From the memoirs of such persons as J. Saunders Redding, one gains a sense of the way in which all Blacks—including the middle class—viewed the prospect of education in an environment which refused to acknowledge their existence. The past experiences of Blacks in white higher educational institutions can best be understood by comparing their experience with those of Asian and African nationalists who studied abroad at the Sorbonne and Oxford.

The continuing war in Southeast Asia, the growing impersonality and bigness of the university, and the rapid television transmittal of techniques of student disruption have had their impact on Black and white alike. Yet, the implications of these phenomena are interpreted quite differently by Black and white student radicals. They may well share common heroes in Guevara, Cleaver, and Fanon, yet there is a distinct difference between the inferences drawn by a student reared in Scarsdale and one reared in Watts. The radical white students may view the Vietnam conflict in terms of an "imperialist venture"; the Black views it as yet another occasion in which Black people are compelled to kill brown people for a country which daily murders, in countless ways, a Black people. The brusqueness of a professor busily engaged in his research may simply confirm a white student's sentiments about the impersonality of American colleges, but to a Black student the same brusqueness taps deep wells of racial memories and is understood and reacted to as "racism." One who listens to Black students commenting on the wild music, jerky dance motions, disdain of style, and dirtiness of dress of white radicals may understand the basic contempt in which they hold the "new left." Black students look back on roaches, rats, and a daily struggle to sustain life. Therefore, they generally come to the colleges with a seriousness of purpose and sense of moral wrong impossible to duplicate in the soul of any child raised in white suburbia. The white student has many choices should his revolutionary fervor wane; the serious Black ghetto student has none. In the academic structure, therefore, his concern for change is not a momentary and romantic fad; it seems to him necessary for the very survival of his people.

The Black assault on the university comes at a time when the university's legitimacy as an institution is under severe and sustained attack from both the right and the left. The white student revolts of the past five years have stripped the Emperor of his clothes and left him exposed—fair game for all who harbored grievances. One is almost tempted to think, in viewing the present scene, that it has become a question of who is to administer the coup de grâce—white students, Black students, or state legislatures? In any case, Black student action takes place in an atmosphere inconceivable to a college administrator a short ten years ago.

Afro-American college students are adolescents, passing through the same identity crisis as any other student; yet, even here, the surface similarities mask deep-seated differences. For, as those who have read Erikson's *Young Man Luther* know, the identity crisis of an individual is reflective of the socioeconomic conditions of his environment. The coming of age of an Eskimo child bears little resemblance to that of a Burmese child. Each is coming to terms with his place in the adult world, but his role in that world is determined by the particular dictates of his society. When the society is being torn apart by internal forces beyond its comprehension and is unable to adjust to new circumstances, the identity crisis frequently manifests itself in open revolt. The present Black student generation was raised in the midst of the most powerful Black protest movement ever mounted in this country. Their childhood heroes were Martin Luther King, Stokely Carmichael, and Malcolm X, all of whom enjoyed enormous prestige among the Black population at large. It is understandable, then, that the Black societal demands on these youth are far different from those on most Blacks of twenty years ago. American Black society expects these youth to bring an end to the slave heritage. Unfortunately, white America is not prepared to accept an identity crisis of such magnitude.

There is little similarity between the "demands" of white and Black students. Whites demand and get sexual permissiveness or representation on faculty bodies, and soon Blacks—or many Blacks—make seemingly irrational demands for a "completely autonomous school of Black and Third World Studies," or a "dean of Black Culture, chosen solely by the Black Students' Union," or "no grades for Black students for two years." It is necessary to examine the assumptions of the Afro-American student movement, and to ask whether the American university, as presently constituted, can respond to what is said and what is really meant. The intensity of Black feelings and the conservatism of the white university may make inevitable the establishment of Northern and Southern Black-controlled colleges as an alternative.

The rationale for the statements made above can only be understood in the historical context of the struggle by Africans in this country to wrench knowledge, and thus power, from a society that had no intention of sharing its wealth with Black people. No comprehension of today's problems can be obtained without an examination of attempts by early Black educators to break the white stranglehold; the attitudes of whites toward the education of Afro-Americans; and the traditional stance of white institutions of higher education toward the Black question. As the history of the century-old educational genocide perpetrated against Africans by white Americans unfolds itself, it is to be hoped that the reader will understand the reasons for the intensity, yes, even ferocity, of the contemporary Black movement for the education of Afro-American youth which will become the focus of our attention in the latter half of this book.

2

Make the Cruel Oppressor Tremble!

The Early Search for a Theory of Black Higher Education

The 1829 "Appeal" of David Walker, the famous Black abolitionist, argued that Afro-Americans must obtain the best education possible.[1]* He himself would crawl on his hands and knees "through mud and mire" to sit at the foot of a learned man because he knew that "for coloured people to acquire learning in this country makes tyrants quake. . . . The bare name of educating the coloured people scares our cruel oppressors almost to death." [2] White Americans realized also, both before and after slavery, that the quantity and quality of the education of Black people was not an abstract philosophy but an explosive question with political and economic implications. Whites never forgot the connection between education and the status of Blacks in America. The structure, content, and accessibility of education to Blacks throughout the century following Emancipation reflect that constant understanding.

In this country in 1865, of some five million Africans, 95 per cent were illiterate, devoid of communal

*Notes begin on page 157.

ties except to a plantation, possessed of no capital, and deprived by national policy of the land to which their labor should have given them title. Many, of course, had been freed men; others had been trained as artisans in carpentry, blacksmithing, and the construction trades. Some had been house servants and many, although proportionately few, had been taught to read and write. As the war ended, white America faced Black people who required education if they were to survive, and if they were, as Du Bois said later, "to receive an income which will insure a civilized standard of living, to make it possible for them to preserve their health; to keep crime down to a minimum and to educate their children; with the eventual object of giving this group sufficient leisure to advance by means of talented people among them in science, art, and cultural patterns." [3]

Winthrop D. Jordan, in the excellent dissection of white attitudes toward Blacks, that repeatedly returns to the white preoccupation with the blackness of African peoples, notes that seventeenth- and eighteenth-century "scientists" began to associate blackness with their darkest and most prurient thoughts.[4] If that blackness could not be removed, then ample biblical, anthropological, and ethical evidence indicated to the white mind an ineludible connection between Africans and all the evil, ignorance, and superstition against which the Protestant ethic had been erected. Blacks were incapable of learning and must be protected from their natural immorality. From this ideological base, it was but a short mental leap to the derivative concepts of African kinship to gorillas and related myths about the animal-like sexual organs in Black men. No human being could possess such characteristics without, in fact, being nonhuman. If, they reasoned, blackness of skin placed an individual in the animal species, then whites were justified in treating such creatures, after taming them, in the same fashion they would treat a dog, horse, or cow. And dogs, horses, and cows do not go to school.

The emerging white image of Africans was suffused with belief in their limited mental capacities; even liberals held to that view:

Now altho' the Negroes might not have the understanding that some other nations have, then I do believe there is less require [of them], and if they do as well as they know, I do believe it is well with them.

—Elihu Coleman, in 1733,
a Boston antislavery person[5]

We may concede it as a matter of fact that [the Negro race] is inferior; but does it follow therefore that it is right to enslave a man simply because he is inferior? This, to me, is a most abhorrent doctrine . . . it would place those who are deficient in intellect at the mercy of those gifted in mental endowment.

—Owen Lovejoy, 1860, Illinois
abolitionist[6]

But never yet could I find that a black had offered a thought above the level of plain narration, never seen an elementary trait of painting or sculpture.

—Thomas Jefferson[7]

Within this context, it is not surprising that the works of the first published Black American writers were scrutinized with a curiosity usually reserved for laboratory experiments. Can a monkey hold a spoon? Yes, a monkey can hold a spoon. Thus, the writings of Phyllis Wheatley, the Black poet, and Benjamin Banneker, the Black inventor and surveyor, received intense attention as the white world tried to decide whether Africans were capable of arranging the English alphabet in such a way as to produce a coherent thought. It was at this time that Pushkin, a Black man, was creating the modern Russian literary language.

The sense of Black mental inferiority was deeply ingrained in the thoughts and actions of those whites who shaped the contours of Black education in the South. J. L. M. Curry, a benevolent white Southerner and agent of the Slater Fund, a major source of financing of Black colleges, stated: "The white people want to be the Leaders, to take the initiative, to have the direct control in all matters pertaining to civilization and the highest interest of our beloved land. History demonstrates that the Caucasian will rule." [8]

The only avenue of escape for captive African peoples in America was through the knowledge contained in books. First, there would have to be federally funded elementary schools in every village. Second, a federally funded group of highly trained teachers would have been sent to those villages. Centers of literacy would have to be established for adult education. This first thrust could have carried through for five to ten years, to be followed by the establishment of regional high schools with both vocational and academic curricula to serve as the funnel through which the most able Black youth would have gone on to federally subsidized colleges. Over a period of fifty or seventy-five years, the educational level of the Africans would have risen to that of white Americans. One need only note that the much maligned and despotic tsars of Russia, when faced with the problem of freeing their serfs, not only gave the peasants land but took major steps toward developing an educational plan to bring them into the mainstream of the society.

Yet it would be absurd to assume that any such educational plan for Africans could have been forthcoming in white America. The obstacles to such a policy were formidable. Even the Abolitionists doubted that Blacks were indeed educable in the Western sense of the word. Their suspicion of inherent African mental incapacity dominated and, indeed, has never vanished from American thought.

White Southerners were unalterably opposed to education for Blacks. Southerners feared that education would lead to discontent with the serfdom they proposed to impose upon freed Blacks. The North had a missionary interest in the Black population, but for whites, Black literacy was far less a priority than the move westward toward Indian territory and the search for raw materials to fuel the Industrial Revolution. For both Northerners and Southerners, moreover, it was apparent that an educated Black would be a dissatisfied Black. Without land ownership, without jobs even in the trades, without a place among the managers of technology, educated men would be dominated by unrest. In consequence, Southern Blacks did not, as a people, receive an education. Henry Allen Bullock, the leading authority on Black education, notes, "In all the South, as late as 1910, there was not a single eighth grade rural Negro public school. No Negro public school, rural or urban, was approved for two years of high school work." [9] The weak educational effort that did exist was rooted in the realization that the Southern economy needed Black labor capable of counting and reading simple instructions. A carefully diluted education would confirm Blacks in their position of subservience to whites: they would know and accept "their place."

There has never been a national commitment to educational opportunity for Black folk.

The white missionaries created industrial-training colleges, under the influence of General S. C. Armstrong, the founder of Hampton Institute, which became the prototype for Black higher education and the recipient, along with Tuskegee, of the bulk of white philanthropic support.

Armstrong felt that the African "is capable of acquiring knowledge to any degree and, to a certain age, at least, with about the same facility as white children; but lacks the power to assimilate and digest it. The Negro matures sooner than the white, but does not have his steady development of mental strength up to advanced years. He is a child of the tropics, and the differentiation of races goes deeper than the skin." [10] He regarded Blacks as childlike, lazy, slothful, and in need of the most rigid and civilizing discipline.[11] Most of those who funded Black education in the South shared this assumption.

Under the impact of intervention by missionaries and such philanthropic bodies as the Rockefeller, Slater, and Peabody funds, a system of primary and higher education developed for Blacks in the South. Institutions called colleges were created, and primary schools began in diverse areas of the South. But it was clear that the colleges were in most cases little more than high schools, and that the general level of education for Blacks, as Du Bois noted, was of low caliber. Some two hundred institutions of higher learning for Blacks were created in the three decades after the Civil War, but only a few were worthy of the designation of "college." They were almost totally bereft of either federal or state support and relied primarily on the largesse of churches and philanthropy. The source of funding was white, the faculties were white, the administrators were white. Over the years between 1865–1935, both Black faculty and administrators placed a continuous and finally successful pressure on the institutions to replace white professors and presidents with Blacks.[12] But in the decades immediately following the war, Blacks concerned with education of their people had few alternatives. If there was to be any book learning for Black children, it had to be on white terms.

There was little comprehension, as there had been in Russia's emancipation, of the possibility that the unleashing of Black intellectual potential would enrich the society as a whole. Rarely in the literature of white thought about Blacks is the possibility explored that the Black intellect could contribute to the development of white society. At the most optimistic level, white society felt that Blacks might possibly serve as the teachers, clergy, and doctors for their own people.

The primary intervention in Black higher education came through the Freedmen's Bureau, in collaboration with the American Missionary Association, which served as the principal impetus to the funding, in the years immediately after the Civil War, of Fisk, Atlanta University, and Talladega. Other religious organizations helped establish Howard, Virginia Union, Morehouse, and Shaw universities. These institutions were to prepare a cadre of Black clerics who would spread the word of God to heathen Blacks. Yet these institutions turned out to be the spawning ground of the Black intelligentsia.

A second constraint on the development of education for Blacks had been white fear of rebellion led by enlightened Africans. The revolts of Toussaint L'Ouverture, Gabriel Prosser, Denmark Vesey, and Nat Turner had seared into the Southern mind the well-founded belief that exposure to books resulted in the creation of dissatisfied and dangerous Blacks. George Tucker, a Virginia slaver, said after Gabriel's bloody revolt, "Every year adds to the number of those [Blacks] who can read and write. This increase of knowledge is the principal agent in evolving the spirit we have to fear." [13]

A Southern editor in 1867 wrote to a white teacher: "The idea prevails that you instruct them in politics and sociology; that you come among us not merely as an ordinary school teacher, but as a political missionary; that you communicate to the colored people ideas of social equality with whites. With your first objective we sympathize; the second we regard as mischievous and only tending to disturb the good feeling between the races." [14]

Although contemporary white experts on Black education,

such as Riesman and Jencks, may well think that Black people were docile, resistance against slavery had been fierce, daily, and determined.[15] Numerous accounts indicate that the prospect and actuality of African resistance dominated the Southern mind both before and after the Civil War. During the Reconstruction, the fear of a truly liberating education for Blacks controlled Southern thought to such an extent as to make it impossible— even if Northern philanthropists would have had it otherwise —to create a system of higher education for Blacks in the South devoted to a knowledge of the social sciences and philosophy with the consequent exposure to Rousseau, the French Revolution, and the ideas of equality so deeply imbedded—as if a private property—in the white mind. All racists—like authoritarians, including Stalin and Hitler—have understood the ramifications of exposure of minds to thoughts that might lead to a questioning of the system which oppressed them. Far better for the South that the education of Blacks be confined to the Bible, rather than venture into studies of the American and French revolutions.

The Northern philanthropists agreed to these Southern conditions of education of Black folk in the same fashion that they had agreed to the elimination of Black civil and political rights, to lynchings, and to the imposition of social segregation. It was decided that the Black people of the South would be educated minimally and vocationally, and that such learning as they received would be subordinate to the educational needs of the white Southerner. It only required a Black voice to articulate the virtues of this system of education. He appeared in the person of Booker T. Washington.

The founder of Tuskegee, a disciple of General Armstrong, Booker T. Washington remains today an enigmatic figure, impossible to place in the niche of either "Black nationalist" or "Uncle Tom." In the heyday of Washington's power, from 1895 to 1905, the majority of Black public opinion supported his program of accommodation. Whether his following was due to his broker function in regard to the allocation of white funds to Black institutions, or to Black belief in his platform, is unclear. In all probability, both factors were important, but overshadowed by the general Black perception of the limits imposed upon

African development by white America. It was during this decade that the great roll-back of Black reconstruction took place. Lynching rose to a bloody peak, the structured segregation was perfected, and the Ku Klux Klan became the dominant political force in the South. Only a slight difference exists between the state of slavery and the state of freedom, and that difference is measured by the variety and quality of alternatives open to a people. For African peoples in America, those alternatives in 1900 were so sparse and few as to approximate slavery. Neither the states nor the federal government intended to finance or even to stimulate the growth of Black education. Black educators, in consequence, had to rely on private philanthropy and the modest tuition fees raised from their impoverished students. The philanthropists, in turn, had to inject funds into Black education on Southern terms, about which there was no equivocation: the education of Blacks should not in any way endanger the political, social, and economic hegemony of Southern whites.

Neither Booker T. Washington, then, nor the mass of Black people were free agents. Even the most militant blacks—Du Bois, for example—shared to some extent the pervasive racist ideology that Blacks were a childlike race in need of great increments of civilization. It may not have been, therefore, opportunism on Washington's part to focus on the short-range and pragmatic goal of eliminating the immediate poverty and illiteracy that afflicted Black people. His aim, in brief, was to provide an education "relevant," as he perceived it, to the needs of Black people. Such an education would be directed toward Black self-sufficiency in a rural environment. It was both an educational philosophy premised on the Protestant work ethic and a nascent form of Black nationalism. Washington had ample precedent for his position. Frederick Douglass, a half century earlier, had focused on the establishment of a skilled farmer and artisan class as the fulcrum for elevation of Black people. In proposing a program for a Black industrial college, Douglass had argued, "The most telling, the most killing refutation of slavery is the presentation of an industrious, enterprising, thrifty, and intelligent free black population. Such a population I believe would rise in the Northern States under the fostering core of such a college as that supposed."[16]

Moreover, throughout the country, vocational and industrial colleges were coming into vogue. Thus, there seemed to be a confluence of several factors in the development of Booker T. Washington's philosophy: (1) his perception that a vocational education was necessary for the mass of Black people; (2) his sense that vocational education was part of a broadly based American movement; (3) his political assessment that the South would not tolerate the growth of a generation of liberally educated "agitators" for racial equality.

Yet, when all extenuating factors are weighed, it is clear that Washington's great sin against Black people was the enthusiasm with which he embraced his obsequious role. In perusing his writings, one finds that, for him, Black children had no potential other than that attributed to them by white society. As an example of this basic sense of African inferiority, one can note these words: "We went into slavery pagans; we came out Christians; we went into slavery pieces of property; we came out American citizens; we went into slavery without a language; we came out speaking the Anglo-Saxon tongue."[17]

Washington reserved his greatest scorn for those Black "agitators," Northern-educated and frequently of light color, who seemed to him to be ignorant of the real needs of Black people. Law, Hebrew, and Greek—these were all useless pursuits when Black people had to be fed and clothed. Moreover, Washington thought the liberal arts implanted all kinds of wrong-headed ideas about equality and justice in the minds of Black people, ideas that only served to alienate Southern whites and create dissatisfaction among Blacks who would have done more for their people by mastering a trade. Thus, one detects in Washington's thought the beginning of a conflict which has its ramifications even today. It is a conflict, emerging unevenly and with many contradictions, between those who would pin the foundations of Black education to the obvious and immediate needs of the Black community, including the rejection of Western liberal arts, and those who see the salvation of the race in the training of Blacks in a broad spectrum of educational endeavors which, by definition, must incorporate some features of the white educational establishment. Washington's view of Black education represents the reductio ad absurdum of the community-oriented education for, if it had taken root, the outcome would have been a race of depoliticized replicas of the white working class, rendered incompetent and incapable of dealing with the political and social injustices which remained the root of the Black situation in white America.

The major opposition to Washington came from W. E. B. Du Bois, who built on the anti-Washington movement begun by the fiery Harvard Phi Beta Kappa graduate, William Monroe Trotter, editor of the radical Black Boston newspaper *Guardian*. Du Bois, it should be emphasized, was not completely in disagreement with Washington. As he articulated and built his educational philosophy, he frequently indicated that most Blacks should receive an education which would permit them to make their daily bread at an honest and skilled job. Indeed, in his autobiography, he pointed out that a prime reason for the low quality of Black higher education in the South had been the belief on the part of the colleges' founders that every Black child could benefit from higher education. To Du Bois, such thinking was detrimental to the long-term interests of the race. He believed, instead, in the theory of the "talented tenth," i.e., that in the Black race as in all other races there was a hereditably controlled elite whose potential would blossom within the proper educational context. The task was to identify these talented persons and give them the best education available. Du Bois, of course, formulated this theory from an elitist educational background of a white Northern high school, two years at Fisk, and undergraduate and graduate training at Harvard and the University of Berlin. Du Bois' primary disagreement with Washington came from his sense that the Tuskegee educator's theories would result in the denial of a liberal education to this "talented tenth" and to the consequent absence of broadly educated Black leaders with the intellectual tools to set the political, economic, and social goals of Black liberation. Through no vehicle other than liberal education could Du Bois envision the creation of a Black counterforce to the racist ideology and practices of the United States. Du Bois' educational philosophy, then, was inextricably connected to an even larger struggle with Washington over the latter's role in maintaining the racial status quo in America and his constant sniping at those Blacks who called for a no-holds-barred struggle against the subjugation of the race.

It would be an oversimplification of Du Bois' thought not to recognize that his view of the quality of education necessary for Black elevation was not limited to the doling out to the "talented tenth" of a traditional liberal arts education. Indeed, his whole life was dedicated to the application of the scientific method to the analysis of the Black condition. While still a young lecturer at the University of Pennsylvania in 1897, he created a detailed and rigorous plan for an examination of the industrial development of Black people in a "typical Southern town." [18] The study would have encompassed the entire political economy of the town's Black population. In his most productive scholarly period at Atlanta University, from 1890 to 1910, he presided over the publications of the Atlanta Conferences which examined every significant aspect of the freedmen's condition. The Black church, the Black college graduate, the Black artisan all received careful scholarly attention. All the studies were focused on real problems and most resulted in projects aimed at eliminating the problems pinpointed by the studies.

In a speech before the organization of Negro Land Grant College Presidents in 1935, Du Bois outlined a brilliant plan for the wedding of scholarship to action. There was, he stated, no reason why "cultivated brains among us" could not apply their talents to the uplifting of their people.[19] He declared that Black colleges should work to train their students for existing needs in the community, but that concentration on specific needs should not result in the denial to students of a broad and cultivated outlook on the world. He called, in addition, for a comprehensive survey of the Black man's needs which would then serve as a springboard to future action and a gauge by which to measure the educational goals of Black colleges. He specifically decried any attempts at creating a Black mythology but instead demanded hard-headed scientific evaluation of the condition of Black people by Black scholars. The detailed curriculum with which he filled the body of this speech—history of the United States, history of Europe, history of Negroes in Africa, South America—outlined a curriculum, both demanding and broad, that was neither a traditional white classical education nor a dead-end vocational track. It stood then, and remains today, as an outstanding effort at creating a "relevant" Black studies curriculum, for neither gambling, pool halls, churches, nor schools would have been absent from the list of activities of Black folk to be examined by Black students and scholars. Nor would the research have been "empty" since resultant plans of self-improvement would have been implemented through all existing organized bodies of Black people. In short, Du Bois' curriculum was a fine blend of theory and action. The scope and refinement of his plan highlights the basic parochialism of Washington's plodding and limited approach to education. Moreover, Du Bois' conceptualization of the educational problem specifically refutes the Washington claim that Northern-bred Black educators had no sense of the real needs of rural Blacks. For Du Bois' work—if it had been realized—would have touched on the life of every Black man, but from a perspective incapable of attainment by those without his sweeping knowledge of academic disciplines and rigorousness of approach to the problems of Black liberation.

In a little-noticed speech of 1933, Du Bois outlined in definitive terms an educational philosophy for American Blacks. No summation can give justice to the breadth and incisiveness of this analysis in which he explored the major questions still before Black Americans. Who, Du Bois asked, should be given an opportunity for higher education? The answer was talented Blacks of *every class* with "brains enough to take fullest advantage of what the university offers." What should be the content of that curriculum? Should it be a copy of that offered at Harvard? "No," said Du Bois, for education for Black people had to originate from the needs of those Black people. This was the one truth that Washington had fastened onto: "It is idiotic to proceed as though we were white or yellow, English or Russian. Here we stand. We are American Negroes." [20] No system of higher education, said Du Bois, despite its aspirations toward the universal, could surmount the fact that it was vested in national needs. "A French university is founded in France; it uses the French language, and assumes a knowledge of French history. The present problems of the French people are its major problems." For Black professors, said Du Bois, it made no sense to assume that they were teaching white Americans when in front of them sat Black victims of the American caste system. Did this mean, then, that Black higher education should not aspire to universalism? No, said Du Bois, but this universalism should emerge from a study of the Black condition and its causes, just as American white higher-education universalism emerged from the socioeconomic base of white America. He summed up his argument: "A Negro university in the United States of America begins with Negroes."

Carter Woodson, founder of the Association for the Study of Negro Life and History, intellectually joined with Du Bois in the attempt to make Black studies the core of the curriculum of Black colleges. In his *Mis-Education of the American Negro*,[21] he declared that it "may be of no importance to the race to boast today of many times as many 'educated' members as it had in 1865. If they are of the wrong kind, the increases in numbers will be a disadvantage rather than an advantage." [22] In Woodson's opinion, the disciplines of economics, history, and philosophy as conceived by white Americans were nothing more than rationales for the caste system in America. Exposing Black youth to such curricula could only, in his view, be detrimental to the interests of the race. Instead, like Du Bois, he insisted that the educational thrust in Black institutions should be directed at the grounding of Black students in matters of African and Afro-American history, economics, and sociology.

Black colleges in the South evolved neither into the vocational institutes desired by Washington nor into the Black catalysts of change proposed by Du Bois and Woodson. Looking back on the establishment of higher education institutions for Blacks, Du Bois suggested that they had been built too quickly and without adequate standards of academic excellence. In his words, "They had scattered haphazard throughout the South some dozen poorly equipped high schools and miscalled them universities." He did not condemn the efforts of those early Black educational pioneers, but felt that they did not, because circumstances would not permit, understand the gravity of the educational uplifting task ahead of them.

The colleges were forced by the allocation of white funds to give more than lip service to the concept of vocational training. Few Black colleges could escape from the necessity of appearing to abide by Washington's philosophy. By 1900, almost half of the 9,000 Black students enrolled in colleges were, in reality, enrolled in elementary or secondary curricula. It could not have been otherwise given the paucity of resources and the almost total illiteracy imposed upon these African people under the slave system. It also cannot be denied that the liberal arts programs that did exist were often watered-down caricatures of white curricula. Most important, the colleges created an environment of accommodation with the Southern caste system that left its imprint on their graduates.

History, however, is never uni-dimensional, nor is the outcome of any attempt at change predictable. Peter the Great, a tsar with a vast intolerance for dissent but faced with the necessity for creation of a technological intelligentsia to build Russia's military might, established institutes that in his opinion would produce loyal state engineers. He found, instead, that even the most technologically oriented curriculum inevitably led to broader and, therefore, dangerous perspectives on the world. Neither he nor subsequent Russian rulers were able to solve the dilemma posed by the necessity for literacy, on the one hand, and political obedience, on the other. His dilemma was finally ended by the Russian Revolution of 1917. The new Russian leaders found themselves faced with the same dilemma, one never yet fully resolved. In the same fashion in the United States, literacy and exposure to books created the rudiments of a Black middle class whose own relative affluence and stability formed the base for the present Black drive toward recognition and power. Washington wanted the Black graduates of his college to prosper and become property-owning burghers. But the same conditions which created the structure and content of Black higher education also dictated that Blacks would be unable to exercise their skills in the areas for which purportedly they were being trained. Thus, Black artisans who had grown steadily in numbers under slavery, had practically disappeared by 1900, the result of the assumption by white laborers of formerly "Black" jobs. The rise of white trade unions with restrictive covenants completed the freezing out of Black artisans. In the same manner, the tenant system of farm labor and increasing mechanization made the acquisition of land almost impossible for trained Black agronomists. The unexpected outcome then of the "vocational-agricultural" thrust of Black education was the movement into high school, elementary, and college teaching of the graduates of Black institutions of higher learning. Unable, by dint of the caste system, to find employment in the "other economy," they went forth into the Black communities of the South on the basic task of teaching reading and arithmetic to their illiterate brethren. Others became doctors, ministers, and petty businessmen—all formed the foundation for the uplift of their race and a movement far different from the social accommodation pattern described by Washington and his white backers. It was primarily through Black college graduates that the literacy rate of Blacks was raised from 68.2 per cent in 1890 to 81.0 per cent by 1930, and this was accomplished in the face of a Southern onslaught on Black education, shrinking state expenditures on the Black population as compared with educational expenditures on the white population. The Black college graduates had heeded Washington's advice "to cast down their buckets" but had brought up books instead of agricultural tools. Black colleges provided a higher educational base, no matter how limited, for the development of a Black bourgeoisie, and the formation of a nascent middle class was crucial in creating the present Black assertiveness. For the Black middle class, thwarted on every side by segregation and deprived of the possibility of movement outside of the caste, was forced to take a relatively radical stance that linked their fate to that of the oppressed Black masses. A consciousness of the unity of Black people was implanted in Black middle-class students by even the most innocuous of curricula.

The Black colleges, moreover, served as a refuge and haven for Black professors intent on the development of Black scholarship. Atlanta University, Fisk, Howard, Talladega, all sheltered Black scholars who in the period from 1900 to 1950 provided the basic intellectual antidote to the venom of racism pouring forth from both Northern and Southern holders of white professorial chairs. Beside the towering figure of Du Bois, others like Carter Woodson, Charles H. Wesley, Horace M. Bond, Alrutheus

A. Taylor, Ralph Bunche, and Luther P. Jackson set themselves to the task of creating a history and sociology of Black folk. Their work stands today and forms the essential starting point for any examination of the evolution of African culture and society in the United States.

In the face of the awesome educational mission performed by the Black colleges, one can only be dumfounded by the intellectual conceit of such white scholars as Christopher Jencks and David Riesman, in their chapter on the Black colleges in the influential book *The Academic Revolution*.[23] Their basic argument, replete with anecdotes and slurring references to Black people, is that the vast majority of Black colleges are an "academic disaster zone" and that even the "best" of such colleges are barely on a par with mediocre institutions across the country. While at some points in their discussion they attribute the cause for this alleged condition to the caste structure of the South, at others they heap blame upon the Black professors, administrators, and students of these schools. Referring to some Black students, the authors declare that they represent a "peculiarly noxious combination of mindless materialism and fundamentalist rigidity."[24] They call some Black professors semiliterate and state that they hear more tales of sexual exploitation of students than they have ever heard on white campuses. The reader is left with an almost unrelieved sense of those Black stereotypes that have always been present in the white American mind.

By Harvard standards, of course, the Black colleges were inferior institutions. But one can only be astounded at the fact that trained sociologists cannot look beyond the surface to the vital function that was performed and is presently being performed by those colleges. For generations, no other colleges admitted Black students. And many of these graduates became the leaders of their people.

The perspective of these academics, as is the case with most white scholars of Black affairs, is skewed by their non-blackness. As children, they were never raised in Black segregated elementary schools where the only teachers were Black graduates of Black colleges. They, therefore, cannot imagine the compassion, force, and energy which those "uneducated" teachers poured into the Black children of the rural South and the Northern ghettos.

They cannot comprehend the frustrations these intelligent people endured and the degree to which they channeled those frustrations into the creative task of educating the Black children who sat in the classes before them, sometimes tubercular, sometimes hungry, sometimes shuddering with thoughts of parents assaulted by whites. Those bourgeois teachers were *Black* bourgeois, who taught Black children pride in their heritage decades before the present crisis over Black studies which is largely the product of educating Northern Black children with white teachers and a curriculum that downgraded and humiliated Black people. Riesman and Jencks, both distinguished white sociologists, never even allude to the stimulating force exerted by Cheyney and Lincoln on the education of Black folk in Philadelphia, or of Morgan, Hampton, Virginia State, and Virginia Union on Baltimore and Washington's Blacks, and so on to small Black colleges in the South, drawing on a population within a fifty-mile radius of the college. Finally, they fail to recognize the role played by the colleges in the development of Black nationalism in numerous Black enclaves of learning as Blacks from all regions of the country came together to know one another and to know, through the interchange of ideas, that theirs was a common problem demanding a common solution. History's outcome is never clear, and the end impact of those "ill-financed, ill-staffed caricatures of white higher education" is yet to be seen. Indeed, the beginnings of the past decade's Black protest were attributable precisely to Black students from Black colleges, whose "sit-ins" set off a movement whose end is still not in sight.

It was apparent that, for different reasons, both the whites and the Blacks who touched on the problem of Black higher education felt that a special kind of education was necessary for Africans in America. The parameters of the dilemma were created by the unwillingness of white America to believe either in the efficacy or desirability of educating Blacks to participate fully and on equal terms in the society. Facing a hostile and unyielding white majority, Black people had to design, with the aid of some whites of mixed motives and with negligible capital resources, a system of self-education. In the midst of widespread economic and social misery, some such as Washington were prompted to work within the system toward immediately visible ends. Others, notably Du Bois, regarded vocational education as self-defeating and believed that the human and financial resources available for higher education should be concentrated on those capable of that degree of conceptualization necessary to create a broad-gauged plan for Black hegemony. Neither Du Bois nor Washington felt, however, that the education, no matter what its bent, should be "irrelevant" to the perceived and expressed needs of Black people. Neither of these builders of Black educational theory would have been pleased with a Black Phi Beta Kappa graduate of Harvard University who turned his total attention to achievement in a white Madison Avenue firm. For basic to both philosophies was the necessity for constant, unremitting attention to the needs of the impoverished mass of displaced Africans.

In any event, neither was able to direct the course of Black higher education. The forces amassed against them were too strong and their own resources too weak. Some Black colleges continued to concentrate on the production of vocational and agricultural specialists for whom there were no jobs in their specialties, while some Black liberal arts colleges subjected their students to copies of white curricula. Both types of institutions were, however, performing the vital task of the creation of an educational base for Black people—"one step backward—two steps forward." Du Bois, Washington, and those "tyrannical Uncle Tom presidents" built better than they knew. Their ideas would reemerge and take on ever greater power when the Black intelligentsia bent to the task—seemingly unchanged over forty years—of utilizing education as a means of alleviating the condition of Black folk in American society.

3

It's Just That Our Entire College Is White!

The Black Question and White Higher Education, 1865–1970

In the past five years, the American university has undergone a battering and sustained assault from each of its traditional constituencies—faculty, students, alumni, and the general public. One of the major causes of the present academic disequilibrium has been the failure of the university to come to grips with the most fundamental problem of modern American society—discrimination based on the color of one's skin. Once the most stable institution in the society, the university is now the center of conflicts so intense and sharp as to endanger its very existence. Men who six years ago would have engaged in endless politicking to be named dean of a college have now fled to research institutes or foundations where they serve as experts on urban higher education. Persons long comfortable in their full-professorial chairs and, until recently, contemplating ten more years of academic-year teaching and summers of relaxing at Martha's Vineyard or the farm in Vermont have suddenly opted for early retirement and departed for tranquil rural campuses with no S.D.S. chapter or few, if any, Black students.

It is no exaggeration, however, to state that if the university
—the self-proclaimed repository of conscience—is incapable of
resolving racial conflict, then there is little hope that the society
at large will be able to do so. If hatred of Black people is so
deeply implanted into the psyche of white Americans that it ir-
revocably determines the attitudes of those educators who are en-
trusted with the shaping of the country's leaders, then one can
have little hope for the future of this civilization. The university
of the seventies will increasingly tend to be a microcosm of
America in the distribution of ethnic groups among its student
body. It will possess an advantage over the society in its ability
to solve racial conflict because students on a campus are not as
yet deeply involved in the business of economic survival, one of
the prime reasons for the racial hatred which pervades the relationships among their elders. The central question concerns
the will of the university to set a model for a society in which
each man would receive his due.

Despite the multiplicity of campuses, there is a communality
of traits among most universities. Thus the reading list of first-
year political science does not vary greatly from institution to
institution; economics professors from Cleveland State meet
with their colleagues from Nebraska and Reed at conventions;
book salesmen pursue Hope College faculty with the same energy they devote to Harvard's faculty, for profit-and-loss statements make no distinction among college board scores of freshman classes, and the basic requirements for a physics major do
not greatly differ from place to place. The federal government
and the foundations, through their concentrated injections of
funds into higher education over the past decades, have created
conditions sufficiently common that a Soviet specialist can feel
as much at home in Austin, Texas, as in Cambridge, Massachu-
setts. The University of Texas professor is certain to find around
him colleagues with graduate degrees from Harvard, Princeton,
and Michigan, and he will use a library whose holdings in his
specialty rival those of more prestigious institutions. At the same
time, highly utilized and profitable educational consulting firms,
offering service in everything from the physical planning of
campuses to the automation of registration procedures to widely

scattered colleges, have provided yet another spur to communality. The technological revolution, in brief, has welded the higher education system into a network with so many shared features that it is not surprising that their clients, the students, find common ground for assaulting the institutions. These institutions were, moreover, white in composition of both their faculties and student bodies until the past decade. As will be seen later, Black scholars in white universities in the forties and fifties were so few that one could almost count them on the fingers of one hand. On the racial question, then, the universities again stood on common ground, reflecting the societal status quo.

Indeed, the entire college tradition of the forties and fifties, that time to which most educators look back with wistfulness, was one of silence and acquiescence in the status quo. The colleges were not, as their spokesmen would have one believe, the conscience of America. They *were* America. They were colleges whose professors lauded Justice Felix Frankfurter as an outstanding example of the American intellectual and quietly explained away this man's bending of the Constitution so as to justify the mass incarceration of Japanese Americans during the war.

In retrospect, there was a frightening unreality about the content of a typical liberal arts education. Freshman after suffering freshman across the country was forced to read through Huxley's essays and Saint Anselm's proof of the existence of God. This "educational experience" took place in a pleasant environment in which racially discriminatory fraternities and athletics were the actual center of life on most campuses. At a time when Hitler, Mussolini, and Stalin had slaughtered millions, political science professors still engaged in long debates about the "political morality" of revolt against tyrants. In this environment, the "kooks"—the Jews—those who in later years would turn out to be the most creative persons, were shunned socially, cast aside, and unnoticed. The campuses in the forties and fifties were mainly populated by bright-eyed Americans whose only area of deep thought concerned the deadly serious matter of obtaining a B.A. to prepare them to take their rightful place in the hierarchy of American business or government. The brightest of them produced brilliant honors theses on "freedom of speech" cases, on sixteenth-century Russia, or trade balances between the U.S. and Europe; but it was these same persons who were to go on to become the architects of Vietnam, the polluting engineers, the TV perpetrators of insults to one's humanity and intelligence. In fact, their immersion into the classics of liberal education and all the exposure to the finest minds in America at Harvard, Amherst, Reed, or Swarthmore had left most with little sense of morality. In the midst of academic "on the one hand" and "on the other hand," few had understood what was right. It was not that they had never thought of moral issues, but that these issues tended to be buried for the most part in such places as *The Republic* and the writings of Rousseau. They could never make the connection between the books and the social reality of America. Yet if one had asked them upon their graduation whether they had been "educated," they would have uniformly answered "Yes." They really believed that the study of Thucydides and Emerson had tempered and liberated their minds; that knowing the relationship of Colonel House to Woodrow Wilson had given them insights into the nature of foreign relations. These were generations raised on the intellectual thought of such as Arthur Holcombe, whose writings on the American Republic are only relieved from absolute tedium by the certainty that the noble Senate, the towering figure of the President, or the great minds of the Supreme Court will rush in to save American democracy just at the moment it is ready to fall prey to dominance by some malevolent interest group. In this somnolent, cloistered, optimistic educational environment —occasionally jarred by a fraternity gang rape, or a rich drunken scion dead in a car accident, or suicide—were most of the leaders of this country nurtured.

To disparage the intellectual climate of the American campus two or three decades ago is not to conclude that it might have been different. For just as no force in the world could have prevented Mao Tse-tung from conquering China, so could no force have moved the American campus off dead center. The universities reflected the social, economic, and political contours of American society as it existed. The U.S. had just defeated an evil foe, been presented with a fine new enemy, and was basking in its beneficence as it set about reconstructing the devastated

Western European continent to create a market for American business. The domestic economy, gearing up to produce cars, refrigerators, and dishwashers for the goods-starved American public, offered limitless financial opportunity to white Americans blessed with a B.A. degree. There was no reason for the campus to be other than it was; it stood in perfect harmony with its economic base.

The obvious key, then, to understanding the American university is to subject it to precisely that type of analysis that has long been devoted to the British, French, and Soviet systems of higher education. In each of these cases, political scientists have long considered the higher education system to be a conscious instrument of state policy. No respectable social scientist analyzing the status of British society would dare to omit the role of Oxford and Cambridge in the development and maintenance of social and hence economic differentiation in England. In the case of the Soviet Union and China, it is obvious that the function of education is to serve the state. Yet, for some curious reason, until recently, commentators on the American system of higher education have never sought to link American colleges to responsibility for the American society.

The answer to this subconscious refusal to analyze the real function of American higher education may rest, paradoxically, in the fact that the university system in this country has been even more closely connected to the needs of the society than some foreign systems. The American university, in typical free-enterprise fashion, has adapted to the needs of various constituencies. It has seldom stood in opposition to the prevailing tone of the country. Oxford, with all its class-consciousness, did spawn the Fabian Socialists, Yale gave us Charles Sumner, the apostle of thrift and capitalism. It is not by chance that American universities have never produced a major theoretician of social change—with the exception of Thorstein Veblen and C. Wright Mills; it was as unlikely a product of the universities as a "whistling crayfish."

Harvard College, it must be remembered, was founded, as were scores of other schools across the country, as an institution in which the natural leaders—e.g., the Winthrops—would be exposed to a mixture of religious and classical training aimed at preparing them to assume their ruling role in society. The second major impetus to American higher education came with the passage of the Morrill Land Grant Act of 1865, providing the base for the enormous expansion of state agricultural and technical schools. The legislation was specifically tailored to the needs of American agriculture and served, according to most thought, as the major spur to the development of the agrarian economy. Finally, in the latter part of the nineteenth century, American universities came under the intellectual influence of the great German universities which stressed rigidity, discipline, and scientific objectivity. The German model was attractive to educators because its emphasis coincided exactly with the ideology of the American Industrial Revolution—work, discipline, and a belief in the boundless potential of technology. It was this mixture of "scientific neutrality" with the already built-in pragmatic tradition of service to particular segments of the society which created a university structure whose finest spokesman would be Clark Kerr in his Harvard lectures.

In noting the extensive connection of the modern American university with government, business, and various interest groups, Dr. Kerr put his finger on the basic aim of these institutions, declaring that a new educational system had "demonstrated how adaptive it can be to new opportunities for creativity, how responsive to money . . . how fast it can change while pretending that nothing has changed at all." [1] He continued: "So many of the hopes and fears of the American people are now related to our educational system . . . the hope for longer life, for getting into outer space, for a higher standard of living, our fears of Russian or Chinese supremacy, of the bomb and annihilation; or individual loss of purpose in the changing world. For all these reasons and others, the university has become a *prime instrument of national purpose*." [Author's emphasis.] [2] Although disturbed by some of the implications of the development of the multi-university, Kerr generally looked upon it and found it good. Some four years later, in 1968, James Ridgeway disclosed just how intimate a relationship had developed among the universities, government, and private industry. His findings demolished, if any had ever believed otherwise, the myth of universities being defined as a "community of books and scholars." [3] Robert Nisbet, a sometime perceptive observer of the contemporary American university, traces its present crisis directly to the build-up over the past twenty years of what he mistakenly labels the "humanitarian impulse" in the academic world.[4] By this, he means the ever-increasing involvement, over the past twenty years, of the university with matters that should not concern it. But one cannot find much of "humanitarianism" in the proliferation of "think tanks" devoted to the study of the best methods of killing Vietnamese or of university-affiliated projects directed at collecting intelligence information necessary to the military for the next "Vietnam." [5] The harsh fact is that the activities of American universities in the past two decades were but a logical extension of their traditional pragmatism. The academic community seemingly had stood firm upon the rock of "scientific objectivity," but in fact, the Harvards, Yales, and Ohio States had always been firm partners of the privileged as the struggles of labor, poor farmers, and Blacks for a share of the American dream were waged, sometimes in the very shadow of their campuses.

No societal structure exists, however, without an ideological camouflage to mask its actual function. And indeed, institutions, like persons, are so complex as to sometimes make it difficult to differentiate between the expressed purpose of an institution and its real purpose. In the case of universities, around the real base of scientific objectivity and utility arose the smokescreen of the "liberal arts tradition" whose most eloquent spokesman was Jacques Barzun, firm defender of the theory that Columbia had no responsibility to the surrounding community. To read the works of Barzun, or the lectures of ex-president Nathan Pusey of Harvard, is to be introduced to a world where the university has as its sole end the development of wisdom in the students it receives. This aim is achieved by exposing the young minds to the best thoughts of Western civilization. And through this immersion in Newton, Saint Augustine, Pascal, Thucydides, and Shakespeare, the youth arrives at a point where his own mind becomes honed, critical, and sagacious.

Now, it would be absurd to argue that unforeseen results ever emerge from this type of educational process. After all, the mixture of books, young minds, and talented professors over a period of four years contains much potential for societal change. Yet, by and large, the concept of liberal education in this country has more often been put to use to explain the virtues than the inequities of this society. This failure to perform the true "liberating" of the mind over countless generations may well be the major cause of the present crisis which threatens to culminate in the dissolution of societal bonds. Nevertheless, it is this emphasis on the development of cultivated minds that serves, in Marxian analogy, as the superstructure masking the combination of vested interests which is the actual basis of that entity known as the university.

Assuming then that the liberal arts tradition functions as that ideology to which all interests represented in the university pledge allegiance, who are the parties that determine the meaning of that tradition and what are their interests? The first and most important is the faculty of the colleges. Encased in a public image of scholarship and the objective pursuit of truth, one finds a group of persons categorized by disciplines, with almost total control over curriculum, teaching methodology, size of classes, content of courses, books to be used, and certification of clientele. Among the best of the faculty one finds rationality, humanity, and scholarly creativity so profound as to mark one's intellectual parameters for life. But such people rarely determine academic policy. And so it is to the others that one must turn to obtain a real grasp of the nature of academia today.

No factor is more dominant in the formation of professorial attitudes than the emergence in the past three decades of highly specialized disciplines in the graduate schools. The increased emphasis on specialization has not only divided most campuses into fifteen or twenty academic departments competing for funds, students, and prestige professors, but has also divided departments into warring groups where behavioralists speak not to traditionalists and specialists on domestic American activities find nothing to talk about with specialists on American foreign affairs. Today's academician rises or falls in accordance with the prestige given him by those in other institutions who share his specialty. This emphasis on expertise has innumerable consequences for the climate of today's colleges. Thus, total immersion in the details of post-Shakespearean drama (1603–40) creates a teacher whose narrow range of knowledge scarcely fits him to appear before a group of freshmen in search of a "liberal education." Indeed, the emphasis on expertise has bred a situation in which certain professors are scarcely qualified to teach survey courses within their own fields. They are simply incapable of relating their particular knowledge to the broader world around them. Moreover, the dreariness, hard work, and denial of life that is the regimen of graduate school does not soon fade from the memories of professors. They must, somehow, justify their own voluntary submission to the five- to ten-year graduate school servitude. The solution is to inspire their undergraduate students to emulate them by exposing the young minds to specialized knowledge far removed from what should be the just concerns of a liberal education.

Professors are a conservative lot. One possible explanation for this attitude is evidence that "well over half the recipients of the doctorate come from families where the father had only a high school education or less—more often less—or held a job low in the occupational hierarchy." In addition, almost half of all graduate deans and faculty, plus a large number of graduate students in a 1960 survey, indicated that the primary motivating factor for achieving the doctorate was the desire "to get a job" rather than to become a "research scholar." [6] The data suggest that the graduate work is not so much a vehicle for the creation of wide-ranging thinkers as it is a means for upward mobility of high-achieving but lower-class youth. Having used the graduate school as means for stepping up the ladder within the existing society, it is hardly likely that many professors would be prone to attack the system that spawned them.

Academics are, in the final count, moreover, the equivalent in modern technological society of primitive tale-bearers. They have both a societally imposed obligation and a self-perceived duty to preserve the cultural heritage and pass it on to future generations. It follows that adaptability to changing conditions is not one of the strong suits of the faculty. Nor are there many aspects of career academic life that would predispose professors to true radicalism. College teaching is among the most selfish professions in the world. One is his own boss, is rarely challenged by most students, possesses good status in the society, and only occasionally is judged on the basis of his teaching performance. The pay is good, the vacations long, and there is seldom a need to make crucial decisions about others and bear the *responsibility* of having made those decisions. Lecture notes build up over time, and with the throwing together of paste-job collections of the original work of others, one can rise rapidly in the profession and be assured of permanent tenure. Professors, of course, often regret—with ever-diminishing intensity—that no piece of original research has resulted from a lifetime of "scholarship." But times buries all pain. Most faculty members publish nothing after they receive their mantle of tenure.

The failure to generate original research in no way diminishes the enormous power wielded by the professoriate. It is a power rooted in the public assumption that the society's values and priorities are being properly transmitted to their children. The society need have no fear on this count. I can scarcely forget a luncheon with several of the most distinguished political scientists in the country. The subject was "war" and one of my colleagues, a world-famous scholar, was reminiscing about a sea battle with the Japanese and laughingly recalling how the "yellow bodies and heads" were scraping against the sides of his aircraft carrier. "That was some fun," he said.

This anecdote simply highlights the fact that professors are human beings. They fight and struggle for power in a way that would astound a hardened and successful mafioso about to send his son off to college to gain "culture." Most academic departments in the country have at least one vicious, usually prestigious senior professor whose pastime is the exiling of young, able, but disrespectful junior colleagues to the nearest state teachers' college. Lifetime tenure does not go to those undeferential in the presence of authority. Were the reader privy to a meeting of a college curriculum committee—the holy chapel of most universities, for it controls course offerings—he would see that the process of obtaining approval for a new course or new curriculum resembles nothing so much as the negotiating process for gaining Allied access to Berlin. In most such academic meetings, the first concern of the faculty delegates is that they display their erudition, the second is that the interests of their department in terms of lines, students, and prestige be protected; the third concern is to give objective consideration to the educational value of a proposed change of academic direction. In the same fashion, the creation of honors seminars, small tutorial classes, or new courses within a department is more likely to be a reflection of the particular interests of a professor than a measured decision on what courses should be offered to students. One has only to pick up the nearest available college catalogue and note the clusters of extremely specialized course offerings to understand that the amount of preparation and time demanded of a professor are major considerations in the decision of that professor to offer a course.

There is a body of faculty members, usually young, or if older, fancying themselves attuned to the latest vibrations of the younger generation, who talk of their commitment to relevant teaching, who are verbally radical about the inequities of American society and in the forefront of the struggle for faculty rights. Their radicalism is most often permeated with self-interest. Thus, although they frequently either instigate or follow student protesters, it very often turns out that they are using the students to achieve faculty ends or self-advancement. The radicalness of such faculty members tends to stop at the point where students begin to show an interest in participating in decisions about tenure and promotion. The liberal veneer disappears completely when such professors are faced with Black questions, for almost inevitably faculty radicals have an intense interest in the maintenance of academic standards and Blacks represent a threat to those standards.

College administrators, or "they" as the faculty call them, are the next major component in the vortex of forces that make up today's university environment. Composed primarily of former faculty members, they are set off from the faculty the moment that the title of "dean" is granted them. Administrators are most differentiated from the faculty by the fact that they, unlike their lecturing colleagues, must daily deal with the real world and bear the consequences of decision-making. They answer to many constituencies, the students, faculty, alumni, and, increasingly, legislatures of the land. In such a context, it is not strange that deans and presidents generally desire more curricular innovations than presently exist and, at the same time, want more order on the campus than either the faculty or students find desirable. The administrators' ability either to implement change or maintain stability, however, has diminished over the past years. If, at one time, a dean's or president's control over the purse and his voice in matters of faculty appointments and salaries provided a basis for influencing change, then it is clear today that such power is shared increasingly by the faculty and, recently, the students. The coming unionization of college faculties will result in an even greater diminution of administrative prerogative. As has been the case with schoolteachers' unions, the primary thrust of the college union effort is directed toward the traditional labor goals of more pay for less work. But more important for the future of colleges are the intricate procedures for appointment, reappointment, or tenuring contained in those contracts, for they are certain to limit severely the ability of administrators to change the composition of their faculties in such a manner as to adapt to varying academic demands upon an institution.

The dedication of administrators to change should not be overstated. If the truth be told, most college administrators would be perfectly content with the status quo were it not clear that the maintenance of the status quo leads to revolutionary instability. College deans and presidents are most happy when the problems before them approximate those they thought would face them when as young scholars they committed themselves to careers in college administration. Such matters as faculty parking privileges, sabbatical leave arrangements, and scheduling of classes are for most administrators the subjects to which they would like to devote their attention. And indeed, these problems do preempt their time when they are not engaged in halting a nascent eruption on campus. Consequently, broad evaluation of administration policy is seldom done by deans and presidents. The very process which would permit them to offer alternatives to the "demands" for change falls victim to their administrative penchant for dealing with inconsequertial details. Those rare administrators who manage to conceptualize strategies for measured change more often than not find themselves and their plans wrecked on the rocks of faculty resistance. For, as previously pointed out, power over personnel policies and curriculum, the two most important vehicles for change, is vested in faculty committees. And within most committees are influential professors to whom work on the committee has become a substitute for scholarly work. Over time, such professors become as expert as Wilbur Mills or the late Carl Vinson in matters of both substance and procedure. Within any university, a cadre of these faculty committee specialists develops and it becomes vital to the survival of any administrator that he cooperate with them, even though the forces which they represent are major barriers to institutional change. Within this context, any administrator who felt that student cries for relevance demanded a new type of teacher—a great folk singer, for example —would face a 90 to 10 probability that a person such as Pete Seeger would be denied appointment as a full professor by the faculty personnel committee on the grounds that he does not possess a Ph.D. degree. Registrars, bursars, librarians, and deans of administration are close behind the faculty in resisting change. Immersed in the symmetry of their figures and requisitions, they instinctively resist any action which, in their opinions, will cause reshuffling of books, tables, or monies. Although seldom vested with tenure as administrators, they, by their control over things mysterious to most liberally educated deans and presidents, enjoy permanent positions.

Surrounded on all sides by immovable objects, administrators—buffeted in addition by the protests of alumni and legislators—tend to cast blame on the faculty for their own difficulties and increasingly begin to speak of the faculty in disparaging terms, thus creating the problem of the mirror image. The faculty, as administrators never seem to understand, is safeguarding faculty interests and will never succumb to change until such time as either disruptions or financial sanctions dictate that change is necessary to their survival.

In sum, administrative work in today's university is thoroughly distasteful. It is not strange that one has difficulty in finding suitable candidates for the position of dean or president, for there is literally no respite from the pressures exerted by groups, all of whom have the power, either physical, economic, or educational, to bring an institution to a halt. Increasingly, those persons best qualified to assume positions of academic leadership refuse such posts because they feel that today's university problems will not yield to even the most rational and dedicated attempts at solution. They have no desire to sacrifice their family life and professional reputation in what, to many, seems a hopeless battle.

The weightiest of the millstones around today's administrators' necks is the students. Our emphasis here is on the white student population in those urban institutions and high-prestige universities which in the past few years have experienced sharp increases in the proportion of Black students in their entering classes. These institutions, such as San Jose State, Brandeis, Harvard, and the City University of New York, have been the primary sites of the clash between the white and Black cultures. Within the white student bodies themselves, it is the radicals, patterning themselves after the Black civil rights activists of the early 1960s, who created the environment into which the new Black students entered.

The change in student attitudes over the past ten years came rapidly. As a young professor in the early sixties, I remember a bright young student in a course on the Soviet Union. His primary concern was the development of the Russian revolutionary intelligentsia, and he was fascinated by the growing radicalization of the intelligentsia in the years between 1860 and the October Revolution. Some years later, I met the student on a street, and he informed me that he had dropped out of a promising graduate school career to join the S.D.S. Some three years later, as if following the Russian script, he became one of the founders of the Weathermen. One recalls other students who, in the course of four years, changed from docile grade "hustlers" into pot-smoking, unkempt dropouts with stolen vocabularies of "m——— f———" pouring out of their mouths in a manner that would have shamed even the most militant Black determined to show that he has not cut off his roots from the ghetto. A glance at one's graduate school notes gives some clues to the reason for this transformation. One sees repeated references to the unchanging monolithic nature of communism, to the benevolent attitude of the United States toward underdeveloped countries, and to a belief in the inevitability of progress and the triumph of liberal democracy over the social injustice in this country. Yet, all these myths have faded away as surely and as inevitably as the Green Bay Packers of the 1960s declined and Bill Russell's age overtook him.

The country, in the past decade, has been in a classical revolutionary situation in which the superstructure of politics and economic institutions remained intact while the underlying social-economic realities of the nation were undergoing sharp changes. It was not by chance that at the point where the contradictions within society had reached their greatest intensity, Kerr gave his series of lectures glorifying precisely those elements in the modern American university most distasteful to the present generation of students.

By now it is clear that there are major inconsistencies within the ideology of the youth. One need not accept Lewis Feuer's analysis of the youth as assassins of their fathers in order to understand that much of their behavior does, in fact, amount to little more than temper tantrums. And it is obvious that in their cries of "relevancy" they fail to understand that previous generations received an education that was extremely relevant to the demands of business and the cold war. Nor do they see that their revolt against technology and the demand for a return to a more pastoral life—best exemplified in the communes—are evasions of life and counterrevolutionary because they turn them away from the one factor that can indeed eliminate all societal problems—technology.

Yet, when one finishes with this and other contradictions—for example, the tenacity of the radical youths clinging to the draft exemptions while Blacks, Chicanos, and poor whites fight and die—a substantive truth remains. Much teaching in colleges is irrelevant because, in blunt fact, it is poor teaching, typified by professors with tattered, yellowed notes and textbooks which, precisely because they must be acceptable to East Tennessee State as well as Amherst, avoid the tackling of any real social issues. On the other hand, the teaching of others is often empty because these professors have succumbed to the demand for relevancy and spend their time on questions which will pass with the next issue of the *New York Times*. Thus, many students have concluded that if this is education, then they can do without it. Their questioning and probing, in turn, force professors to face the reality that they are often defending the indefensible: the self-evident reasons for learning their discipline; the need to read texts which add little to the education of a student. The end product of this challenge to professors is that they themselves begin to doubt the necessity for their existence, and this in turn leads to the acceptance by some faculty members of the fact that they are parasites in the educational process, with little more to contribute than the students themselves. The infection of self-doubt among the faculty has led to the tumbling of all the old dogmas about the teacher–student relationship and to the schizophrenic behavior whereby faculty have contributed to the very process of discord which, if uncurbed, will destroy the university and them along with it.

The student strikes, bombings, and sit-ins, and the erratic behavior of faculty and administrators simply tell us that the basic consensual environment which existed before 1964 has broken down and that no new contract among the constituent parts of the university has evolved. It was into this environment that most of the Black students now on white campuses were thrust. It was a situation of sharp polarities and divisiveness as students, faculty, and administrators fought for power over curriculum, budgets, and personnel evaluation. Inevitably, the Blacks demanded a share of this power. As will be seen, the permissive atmosphere and the precedents of sit-ins and disruptions first engaged in by white faculty and white students was to be utilized by Blacks for a purpose with which neither faculty nor the majority of radical students could agree—the granting of power to a group of students whose aspirations and sense of education were alien to the entire white academic community. It was not the first time in history that liberal reformers have been trapped by their own rhetoric.

Nothing reveals the direct connection between American higher education and the operating principles of American society more than the record of white universities in regard to the Black question over the one-hundred-year time span between Emancipation and the beginning of open admission efforts in the mid-1960s. There can be no charitable explanation for the almost total exclusion of Blacks from the faculties, student bodies, and curriculum of these colleges. Nor can there by any justification for the role that these universities played in creating a scholarly rationale for the caste system that emerged over the past century. Little can be gained by punishing the white educational structure for its past actions, but the extent to which the American university tradition was an active ally in the national policy of repression of African peoples should be made absolutely clear.

Basic characteristics of educational racism became imbedded in white colleges and formed the environment where present-day Black students are expected to be educated. The recruitment by white colleges of Black faculty members, the promulgation of racist dogma by white academicians, the historical record of white colleges in recruiting Black students, and the experiences undergone by those students on white campuses provide keys to the understanding of the situation.

One may ask, "What could the colleges have done?" The answer is simple: from 1865 onward, the colleges could have been the vehicle by which a multiracial society might have been attained. By active recruitment of Black students, they could have created a situation in which Black professionals of every order —doctors, lawyers, physicists—would have been at least proportional to the numbers of Blacks in the population at large. They could have brought Black faculty into their colleges in numbers sufficient to have created the image of integrated faculties at the very center of the culture of American civilization. They could have granted Du Bois, Woodson, Wesley, and Locke the prestige and research facilities that would have kept ill-intentioned and badly informed whites out of the business of defining the Black man and his role in this society. Finally, they could have sent forth to their students and to the school systems of this country a steady and unswerving message that Black people are human. The universities, of course, did none of these things, and could not because they were inextricably tied to the nation's socioeconomic base.

The easiest and most obvious means of conveying academia's attitude toward the racial caste system might have been the appointment of Black professors to their faculties. Yet, almost no white institution of higher education in this country, before the hiring of Allison Davis at the University of Chicago in 1941, believed that any Black man was intelligent enough to be a professor at a white university.[7] In 1940, there were 330 Black Ph.D.s in the country. Not one taught at a white university. In an attempt to boost the number of Black faculty in white institutions, the Julius Rosenwald Fund, in 1946, wrote a letter to some five hundred college and university presidents in the North, requesting that they make some effort to recruit Black faculty.[8] Four-fifths of the colleges did not deign to reply to this outrageous request. Most of the colleges that did reply stated that they would make no special effort to recruit Black faculty members. Some said that Black faculty were most needed in Black colleges, others stated that Blacks would be unhappy in the white environment. One said in a classic non sequitur that the Ohio River was too close by to permit hiring a Black faculty member, while one honest college stated that: "It isn't that we discriminate against the Negro race as such, it's just that our entire college is white." Imperceptible progress in achieving the goal of faculty racial integration was accomplished over the two decades following the hiring of Allison Davis.[9] Indeed, by 1960, there were no more than two hundred Black faculty members in white colleges throughout the country.[10] Harvard and Yale, pacesetters in this as in every field of higher education, had no Black tenured faculty members in their liberal arts colleges until ten years ago.

The university was no less racist in its self-defined role of preserving and transmitting the values of the society. The works of leading white scholars have reflected the racial norms of America and have provided an intellectual rationale for the national policy of oppression of Black people.[11] This activity has taken three forms: outright scholarly defense of white supremacy; a "benign neglect" of the Black condition, particularly in textbooks, and intervention into Black matters by the new "experts," liberal white scholars.

In the first category of active support for the theories and practices of white supremacy falls the work of historians such as William A. Dunning, Albert Bushnell Hart, Allan Nevins, Henry Steele Commager, and Claude Bowers; sociologists Howard W. Odum and Robert E. Park; political scientists Frederic A. Ogg and P. Orman Ray; and literary critics Allen Tate, Robert

Penn Warren, and Donald Davidson. The scholarly endeavors of these men underpinned the curricula of high schools and colleges, providing much of the intellectual framework for the education of American adults in the first half of this century. The total impact of their work cannot be overemphasized, for their work was used not only in college classrooms, where future teachers of Blacks and whites were being educated, but also as sources to which writers of textbooks for elementary, junior, and senior high schools turned for their material on Black people. As late as 1961, a survey of high school textbooks indicated that the findings of an earlier 1949 American Council on Education Study on the treatment of Blacks in secondary school textbooks remained valid: references to Blacks, if any, were devoted to the period before 1876 and typically cited the usual white stereotypes about Blacks.[12] Thus, today's university chancellors, police chiefs, publishing house executives, professors of sociology, and mayors of small American towns alike were reached by diversely worded scholarly messages of the inferiority, laziness, incompetence, or childlike nature of the Black man. And hundreds of thousands of today's Black adults were never spared the humiliation, as children, of having their people depicted as an inferior species of mankind.

In *Reconstruction: Political and Economic,* William A. Dunning, professor of history at Columbia University, laid the groundwork for the historical myth that slavery had not been an oppressive institution and that the attempt to give Blacks status as American citizens through the 14th and 15th Amendments was a tragic mistake, as evidenced by the Reconstruction era.[13] The Reconstruction, according to Dunning, was "a social and political system in which all the forces that made for civilization were dominated by a mass of barbarous freedmen." [14] In 1929, Claude Bowers, an eminent journalist, historian, and diplomat, justified the "Compromise of 1877" signaling the end of federal protection of Southern Blacks and the rise of white supremacy in the defeated Confederate States.[15] Of one master's slaves, he says, "great numbers [of them], fat and contented, worked in house and field, grinning in the sunshine and warmly attached to an indulgent master." [16] He refers to the Southern legislatures during Reconstruction as "monkey-houses" and applauds the return of civilization to the South, the end of Reconstruction, and the end of the period when "overtaxed and underprotected whites . . . lived in a state of terror and women were not safe in the streets." [17]

Some fifteen years later, in their *A Short History of the United States*, Allan Nevins of Columbia University and Henry Steele Commager of Amherst were to say of the Reconstruction period that "recent slaves, whose grandfathers had perhaps been African savages, who could not read a line of print, and who had spent their whole lives in the cotton field, were given a full voice in choosing public officers and making laws." [18] They go on to declare that the governments established by the Blacks "were probably the worst that have ever been known in any English-speaking land." The poor downtrodden white Southerner was "in despair"—"but not for long. Little by little the self-respecting whites of the region gained the right of ruling themselves. In part they did this by violence and intimidation. They set up the Ku Klux Klan, which compelled many carpetbaggers to return to the North and frightened Negroes away from the voting places." [19]

Reviewing the entire period 1850 to 1877, they found it "an almost unmixed tragedy" that could have been avoided had the slaves been gradually emancipated, thus sparing "the nation the six hundred thousand vigorous young men who lost their lives in the conflict and the millions of children they would have brought into the world." [20]

Such sentiments were echoed in the widely used *Essentials of American Government* by Professors Frederic A. Ogg and P. Orman Ray.[21] After some discussion of devices like literacy tests, poll taxes, and "grandfather" clauses, used to exclude Blacks from the ballot box, Ogg and Ray concluded that "the heavily outnumbered white populations (in several of the states) must be conceded to have the logic of cold facts largely on their side. The initial mistake was made when the freedmen were enfranchised *en masse* upwards of seventy years ago." [22]

White scholars, of course, reinforced prevailing stereotypes about the nature of the Black mentality. Harvard's Albert Bushnell Hart wrote that, "The theory that the Negro mind ceases to develop after adolescence perhaps has something in it," [23] and

Howard W. Odum, chairman of the sociology department at the University of North Carolina, and president of the American Sociological Society in 1930, noted that Black people were "shiftless, untidy, and indolent . . . dishonest and untruthful." [24] Harvard University saw fit to grant Odum an honorary LL.D. in 1939.

Robert E. Park, the renowned sociologist at the University of Chicago, a white liberal who in the words of Oliver Cromwell Cox was "still strongly opposed to any definition of Blacks as equal to whites," [25] wrote that the characteristics of Black people "manifest themselves in a genial, sunny, and social disposition, in an interest and attachment to external, physical things rather than to subjective states and objects of introspection, in a disposition for expression rather than enterprise and action." [26]

Deeply influenced by Sumner's dictum that mores cannot be reformed by law, Park dismissed any thought that the position of Blacks in the South was due to racist feelings among the whites, but said: ". . . the Negro is quite all right in his place. And that place, like the place of everyone else, is the one to which tradition and custom have assigned him." [27]

In 1930 literary counterparts of the social scientists and historians, Allen Tate, Donald Davidson, and Robert Penn Warren, in collaboration with others, wrote a defense of segregation and a celebration of the "remarkable society" [28] of the Old South with its highly structured relationship between white patricians and Black slaves. Robert Penn Warren said: "In the past, the Southern Negro has always been a creature of the small town and farm. That is where he still chiefly belongs by temperament and capacity; there he has less the character of a 'problem' and more the status of a human being who is likely to find in agricultural and domestic pursuits the happiness that his good nature and easy ways incline him to as an ordinary function of his being." [29] The question before these men was how to preserve that old genteel society. The answer came from Allen Tate. The "answer is by violence," [30] he said.

In a later work, Tate became even more specific about his attitude toward Black people: "I argue it this way, the white race seems determined to rule the Negro race in its midst; I belong to the white race; therefore I intend to support white rule.

Lynching is a system of weak, inefficient rule, but you can't destroy lynching by fiat or social agitation; lynching will disappear when the white race is satisfied that its supremacy will not be questioned." [31]

Donald Davidson, professor of English at Vanderbilt University from 1920 to 1937, another of the authors, declared in a panegyric to rural Georgia: "Lynchings, the work of hotheads and roustabouts, were regrettable, *but what did a few lynchings count* [author's emphasis] in the balance against the continual forbearance and solicitude that the Georgian felt he exercised towards these amiable children of cannibals." [32]

These major writers seem to have agreed that segregation should be preserved, in Malcolm X's terms, "by any means necessary."

These same men went on to form the school of literary criticism known as the "New Criticism" which has dominated the approach to literature of English departments throughout the country over the past thirty years. The approach—arrogant, cold, and disdainful—had at its core the belief that the perfection of form in literature was more important than its content. Thus, no attention was to be paid to either moral or social considerations in the evaluation of literature. Allen Tate could therefore say in his preface to Melvin B. Tolson's *Libretto for the Republic of Liberia* that Black poets were limited "to provincial mediocrity in which feelings about one's difficulties became more important than poetry itself." [33] Yet it was men such as Tate—editors of important journals, with disciples throughout the country—who became the intellectual arbiters of American literature for three decades. The Southerners, defeated in the war, recouped their battlefield losses by establishing strongpoints in the academic world from which their ideology of the innate inferiority of Black people could be launched.

Yet the "benign neglect" of the Black issue by white scholars in the universities was, and is, more widespread than the outright depiction of Blacks as inferior. Textbook after textbook has buried the Black American's condition in a single paragraph or in mere sentence references, amidst paeans to the perfect democracy in which we live. The Black man is the one piece of the puzzle that does not fit. Textbook writers solve the dilemma by pronouncing the puzzle complete and tossing away the offending piece.

For example, the *Elements of American Government,* by John H. Ferguson and Dean E. McHenry, contains in its index no reference at all to Black people.[34] Some two pages are devoted to the poll tax and literacy tests, but the major mention of Blacks comes when the authors state, burying Afro-Americans among other groups, that "the greatness of America is due in large measure to its successful utilization and amalgamation of the genius inherent in the various racial strengths which make up the population." [35] Probably the most widely used textbook in American government, *American Democracy in Theory and Practice,* in its 1951 edition, spread the plight of Black Americans throughout the book, describing, matter-of-factly but with few judgments, the various forms of discrimination that affected Afro-Americans.[36] By 1963, the book's approach to the subject of Black people had been somewhat altered, but there was little that would be offensive to Southern colleges. Referring to the infamous three-fifths compromise over the counting of slaves for taxation and representation purposes instated at the Constitutional Convention of 1787, the authors categorize as "extremists" those Northerners who would have sapped the South's political power by not counting slaves.[37] In their fourth chapter, entitled "A Constitution Intended to Endure for Ages to Come," they spend forty-eight pages glorifying the Constitution which provided "the basis for . . . a more perfect union" without once noting the irrelevance of this document to Black people.[38] Later, describing the Congress, which "mirrors the American people pretty well," they note that Blacks have been underrepresented in Congress. "But whether sex, religion, or race are relevant bases for the election of legislators in a democracy is a controversial issue." [39] The brief section that does deal with Black Americans is timorous: "Because of the inferior education they had received in segregated schools, Negro school children were not always ready to be placed in fully integrated school situations and required to compete with white children of the same age or grade." [40] In their final chapter they note the acuteness of the racial problem and the necessity for its solution, but fall, all the same, into the gradualist pose that "Negroes and other minority groups have been brought into the main streams of American life in ways that would have seemed impossible two or three decades ago." [41] They conclude that this process, however, "cannot be achieved by legal fiat alone and it cannot be achieved overnight." So much for ringing moral affirmations. One need not belabor this point, but a perusal of such a seminal work in political science as *The Governmental Process*,[42] by David B. Truman, shows the same reluctance on the part of the author to highlight the exclusion of Blacks from the American political process.[43]

When certain white scholars did turn their attention to the Black condition, it boded no good to the Black community. Daniel Patrick Moynihan is, of course, the prime example of this syndrome, but there are others, less famous but nevertheless influential, who have typified the liberal approach. Following the publication of his book *Negro Politics*, [44] which involved extensive interviewing of Black leaders in Chicago, James Q. Wilson was appointed associate professor of government at Harvard, where he specialized in urban affairs. His position at Harvard automatically thrust him into a role as one of the nation's leading experts on Black people. By October 1967, this "expertise" had led him to publish an article in *Encounter*, where he dwelt on the causes of and solutions to Black rioting. While he did not wholly discount the influence of social conditions, he essentially blamed the victims for willing and desiring the riots. For example, he wrote that for many young black males "a display of mass violence" had "not only become legitimate but important." He cited unnamed informants who claimed that the younger Blacks are "not only ready for violence, but eager for it." [45] He went on to fault many in the poor Black community for finding "life on the street corner more attractive than life in the factory"; hustling was, for many of them, "more stylish" and "more expressive" than a job.[46] Wilson moved on to the heart of his solution to the problem of riots in Black ghettoes: "Distasteful as it may be, I believe we are going to have to garrison our major metropolitan areas, at least during the summer months, with National Guard Units stationed in armories and available on one hour's notice." [47]

This is one liberal's answer to the American dilemma. It is but a step removed from cordoning off the ghettos and establishing a pass system for their inhabitants, a concentration camp in every city.

Dr. Wilson's former colleague Edward C. Banfield, a chaired professor of urban government at Harvard since 1959, who has recently moved to the University of Pennsylvania, holds similar views on Black people. Banfield's book *The Unheavenly City* [48] is a classic example of blaming the victims. For Banfield, the nation must understand that "lower-class" people find poverty "satisfying." [49] Segregated communities may, in fact, be more the result of the Negro's "having cultural characteristics that make him an undesirable neighbor" than the result of white prejudice. [50] While Banfield denies that "lower-class" is to be equated with Negro, [51] the book effectively does so. There is no substantial race problem in America, but only a *class* problem. And the sooner Black people understand that the major deterrent to their advancement lies in their own cultural patterns, not in racism, the better off the Black community will be: "Like every specialist, the Negro leader is prone to magnify to himself as well as to others the importance of his specialty, seeing every problem in terms of it." [52]

The crux of the problem lies, for Banfield, in the fact that the lower classes are "present-oriented" rather than "future-oriented." He offers a variety of creative solutions to the problem. Thus, a way out for underachieving "lower-class" students in high school is for the age for leaving school to be lowered to fourteen. Again, he proposes that lower-class children be bought and sold to remove them from undesirable families. This, he says, is "as a matter of logic, the simplest way to deal with the problem—and one which would not involve any infringement of parents' rights." [53] While he discarded this proposal as "wrong," he had ceased to be troubled by this difficulty when he put forward the solution again in a *New York Times* "op-ed" piece six months later entitled "The Cities: Babies for Sale." [54] He goes on to propose deliberate abridgment of the freedom of those who would be judged to have higher "probability" for the commission of crime. These persons are described as "undeterrables," and the abridgments suggested are posting a peace bond, observing a curfew, liability to search, inability to ride in a private automobile, sequestering in a small town, or, at a more extreme level, confinement to a penal village. Banfield's approach boils down to: Let them eat lead poison.

Another example of the liberal solution is expressed by Nathan Glazer, coauthor with Moynihan of *Beyond the Melting Pot*, [55] a book which, although full of slurring references to Blacks, was accepted by the intellectual community at the time of its publication as the final word on the urban problem. Glazer, too, found his way to the pages of *Encounter*, where he strongly argued that Black people in the country have not suffered a "unique deprivation." [56] Maybe a little bit, says Glazer, but certainly not enough to explain by itself "the special quality of despair and hysteria that now dominates much Negro political discourse." [57] Glazer regrets that Blacks are suddenly violating the American ethic by demanding quotas and is particularly disheartened by Black declarations that universities and corporations are racist. Joining Wilson, he states that nothing the federal government could do would satisfy Black aspirations and, therefore, concludes that it is time for a more gradual approach to the problems of Black people. Four of the nation's leading white urbanologists—Moynihan, Banfield, Glazer, and Wilson—were agreed about the nature of the urban crisis.

The historical record of white colleges in admitting Blacks to their student bodies is no more encouraging. The history of Blacks in white colleges begins in 1826, when the first Black college graduate was given his degree at Bowdoin College. By 1910, some 693 Black students had graduated from white colleges, the bulk of them after 1890.[58] From 1826 to 1890, only thirty students had been graduated from all-white colleges, if one excepts Oberlin, which had graduated some fifty Black students before 1890. By 1910, with the exception of Oberlin (which dominated all statistics with a total of 149 graduates), Dartmouth had graduated 14 Blacks, Harvard 41, Penn 29, Kansas 60, Yale 37. The rest of the students were parceled out in ones or twos among other colleges. Typical of the admissions policy was the fact that the City College of New York, founded as an institution to serve the poor, had a total of two Black college graduates by 1910.

Over the following four decades, Blacks in small numbers were constantly graduating from white colleges. But by 1954, only some 4,080 out of 480,000 college freshmen entering white colleges were Black.[59] There was no concerted effort by white colleges to admit Black students. The basic attitude of many white institutions emerges in replies to a Du Bois survey of 1910:

Princeton University has never had any graduates of Negro Descent. Yale University has never tried to attract Negro students and, on the other hand, has never felt justified in refusing admittance to those who become qualified to enter.

Fordham has had no applicants for admission from the black race. What we should do were the applicants to come, I just cannot say.[60]

In short, white universities felt no special mission, as centers of American culture, to incorporate the former American slaves into that culture. A small group of Blacks were exposed to white higher education from 1900 to 1960, and their impact on the condition of their people is not to be underestimated. But, more germane to our examination of higher education for Blacks— for it presages the causes of Black dissatisfaction with white higher education today—is the experience of Blacks in those white ivory towers.

I have already referred to the intense social pressure upon my Black schoolmates and myself after being admitted as the first of our race to a hitherto all-white campus. My own experience "integrating" a small, prestigious college in the flatlands of Ohio was little different from those of Black students years earlier or ten years later. Central to all these experiences was a sense of spiritual and emotional bifurcation. Whether the students were children of slaves at the University of Kansas, students at Harvard, or isolated Black athletes on some prairie campus, the situation and their reactions to it did not differ.

First, they felt pride in being among the small number of Blacks to attend a white institution of higher education. One need only talk to 1920 and 1930 graduates from Iowa, Harvard, Amherst, or Yale to understand the deep sense of accomplishment they still feel in having completed their education there rather than at a Black institution in the South. Usually, as was true of Du Bois describing his experiences at Harvard, the emphasis in these positive memories is on the intellectual climate of those white institutions, a feeling perhaps best conveyed by William Melvin Kelley, describing Blacks at Harvard in the late fifties: "At Harvard, and at any other Ivy League School, the Negro not only loses his Negro consciousness or at least the sore edge of it, but perhaps will acquire something else: the opportunity to develop a certain aristocratic attitude even toward white men . . . he comes to believe, in a quiet way, that Harvard is the best school in the country and therefore he is one of the select. Yale Negroes feel the same about Yale; Dartmouth Negroes the same about Dartmouth, and so on." [61]

Frequently, one meets older Black graduates of such institutions to whom life has been unkind but who still reminisce with a glow in their eyes about their distinguished white classmates who have gone on to great fame. Those Blacks who attended white institutions often regarded themselves as part of Du Bois' "talented tenth." It was their duty to assimilate the knowledge acquired and then use it for the uplift of the Black masses.

A natural concomitant of this pride was an almost inevitable attitude of deprecation toward other Blacks. Thus, Kelley's description of Harvard in the late fifties contains several allusions to the basic distaste among the Black Ivy elite for the street Black. The same feeling overcame J. Saunders Redding in his days at Brown, where he confessed, "I hated and feared the whites. I hated and feared and was ashamed of Negroes. (The memory of it even now is painful to me.)" [62]

Blacks had to understand that they were still considered Blacks by their white classmates and white society at large. Orde Coombs, a contemporary Black writer, referring to his experiences at Yale in the early 1960s, made a valiant, racially motivated attempt to convince two white Southerners that Blacks could think: "One was in my French class. Every question he missed, I answered. I made sure of this by studying French grammar late into the night. And to what avail? To convince one Southerner that a black man knew more French than he did." [63]

George Davis recalled the life of a Black student on a "small liberal arts" campus: "for four years he had felt distant and detached in this fragile, alien environment . . . . the white students looked about the same as the ones he had known. . . . They were still the same healthy, unmenaced children of the rich who had made his life so lonely for four years." [64]

A former student at Kansas State College in the mid-twenties, Frank Marshall Davis summed up the dilemma in a poem:

Giles Johnson, Ph.D.

Giles Johnson
had four college degrees
knew the whyfore of this
the wherefore of that
could orate in Latin
or cuss in Greek
and, having learned such things
he died of starvation
because he wouldn't teach
and he couldn't porter.[65]

Repeatedly throughout the literature one finds escapes from the psychological pressures of the white colleges—either frequent weekending in nearby Black communities, or informal or formal Black social groups organized on the white campus in order to compensate Black students for their almost total ostracism. It is not an accident that one of the first Black fraternities, Alpha Phi Alpha, was formed at Cornell University in 1906. Students at Kansas during the same period spent so much time in the Black community that it began to tell on their classwork.[66] At institutions where there were sufficient numbers of Blacks to occupy a full table, Black corners appeared. Such was the case at state universities where the number of Black students was large: Richard L. Plautt, former director of the National Negro Scholarship Services Inc., said in 1954: "Where they are present in large numbers, there is often a tendency for them to build their own social ghettos. The observation has been made again and again that in large universities, particularly in the Middle West, a 'Negro corner' is conspicuous in the University dining halls and cafeterias." [67]

The same tendency was observed among Black athletes in white colleges in the mid- and early 1960s. Students on white Ivy League campuses in the early thirties visited Boston and its Black section during weekend respites from the tension of life on those hallowed grounds.[68] Understandably, the human toll on sensitive young Blacks living this divided existence was great. No one can count the actual number of lives sacrificed in this effort to get the white man's education, but J. Saunders Redding, writing of his Black roommate at Brown, said that "he was the first of five suicides in a half dozen years from that group I knew in New England." [69] "That group" comprised fifteen Black students.

One can begin to derive a better perspective on the predicament of the Blacks in these colleges if one looks at their situation in terms of the general experience of the creation of intelligentsia in undeveloped countries. In mid-nineteenth-century Russia, a group of people, mainly from lower-middle-class backgrounds and not far removed from the peasantry, gained access to higher education through the various mechanisms of educational reform that accompanied the freeing of the serfs. These persons, the "intelligentsia," became the vanguard of the Russian revolutionary movement to eliminate the poverty of the Russian peasantry. Yet, it soon became clear that the intelligentsia was beset with contradictory views about the peasantry. On the one hand they had to view the peasantry as the base for the revolution, and this, in turn, led to a glorification of the peasant virtues of spontaneity, closeness to nature, and a general lack of contamination by civilization. The intelligentsia soon found, after repeated attempts at inciting the peasants to revolt, that the village folk were essentially conservative. A split developed within the revolutionary movement; some segments proclaimed the potential for village revolutions; others, formerly attached to this notion, proclaimed the necessity of destroying the peasant virtues and introducing the countryside to industrialization, necessarily accompanied by discipline. The latter group evolved into the Bolshevik party. A love–hate syndrome begins to emerge in the intelligentsia's attitude toward the peasantry.

When the intelligentsia from underdeveloped countries are exposed to Western education in Paris, London, or the United States, they are impressed with the totality of the scientific and intellectual resources which permitted the West to colonize three-quarters of the world. They become convinced that the only way for their own countries to attain power is through the creation of a similar technological base. The intelligentsia soon are in conflict within themselves between the agrarian and communal-based societies from which they come and the hierarchical, structured, and disciplined demands of technological development. Thus, national customs, music, and art are emphasized, while at the same time governments headed by Western-educated members of the intelligentsia create mechanisms for the destruction of the traditional way of life. No matter how beautiful the memories of the simplicity and warmth of the traditional ways, the demands of modern society dictate an end to that way of life in the interest of providing a nation's people with the health and economic benefits of technological development.

One finds much of the same schizophrenia among Blacks exposed to white institutions of higher education. Speaking of Harvard's Blacks, William Melvin Kelley said, "With one breath, the Ivy League Negro will ridicule him [the lower-class Negro man and woman] for his lack of taste, the flashy and revealing clothes of his woman, his 'dese, deys, dem, and doses,' and with his next breath he will envy him for his apparent love of life, his woman's Africanesque or exotic beauty, and believe it or not, his rough and ready sexuality." [70] Carter Woodson, a product of white schools, experienced this duality—while on the one hand he was angry that Black and white schoolteachers made "pupils to scoff at the Negro dialect," on the other, he could mock the "dialect" when it issued forth from a Black faculty member and could further say that in a Black studies program, "we would not neglect to appreciate the unusual contribution of Thomas Jefferson to democracy." [71] This recurring theme of the bifurcation of soul, almost constant throughout the experience of Blacks on white campuses, appears in even more exaggerated form when the Blacks, as in the case of many athletes from the ghetto, shared few of those upwardly-mobile aspirations of most Blacks previously admitted to white instiutions. [72]

Despite the psychic and social traumas suffered by the token Blacks in these white colleges, few were "whitewashed" intellectually. Exposure to a curriculum designed for whites and controlled by whites did not result in the graduation of a group of raceless men with no consciousness of the necessity to work for the upgrading of the entire Black population. According to Howard Thurman, the distinguished dean of Boston University's

School of Theology, the influx of highly trained Blacks from white Northern schools into the South was of incalculable benefit to the Black masses: "When young Negro teachers began saying these things to us, the possibilities of higher education extended." [73]

A long line of Blacks, including Du Bois and Robeson, emerged out of a white educational context. Writers whose grasp of the Black condition and concern for poor Black people was equal to that of any of today's Black writers had diplomas from white colleges. A short list suffices to make the point: Jean Toomer was a product of the University of Wisconsin and City College of New York; Rudolph Fisher received his undergraduate education at Brown University; Wallace Thurman was educated at the University of Southern California; Arna Bontemps at Pacific Union College of California; Claude McKay spent two years at Kansas State University; Countee Cullen was a product of New York University and Harvard; Sterling Brown of Williams and Harvard; Robert Hayden of Wayne University and the University of Michigan; Margaret Walker of Northwestern and University of Iowa; Carter Woodson, the founder of the Association for the Study of Negro Life and History, was educated at Berea, University of Chicago, the Sorbonne, and Harvard; Alain Locke at Harvard, Oxford, and the University of Berlin; Katherine Dunham, the preserver of the Black dance tradition, was trained at the University of Chicago; Rayford Logan at Williams and Harvard. In short, there is little evidence to support the view that exposure to white educational institutions created a group of "Oreos." Many graduates of white institutions did indeed take on a "noblesse oblige" attitude toward less-privileged Blacks, but many also felt compelled to turn their energies toward the race. To have been plunged into a white educational environment and to still remain Black created a subtle but forceful dialectical process. Instead of preparing Blacks to be content to enter the mainstream of American life, the white educational structure created its antithesis—Blacks all the more aware of the contrast between the ideals of America and the condition of the Black masses. Far from "whitewashing" the Black students, Harvard created the intellectual counterforce, in Du Bois and Trotter, necessary to overcome the accommodationist Booker

T. Washington. The Ivy League produced the cadre of Black scholars who would go on to form the academic foundations for Black analysis of African and Afro-American studies. The intellectual outcome of the limited effort to educate some Blacks in white colleges was out of all proportion to the numbers.

Before the beginning of the large-scale entry of Black students into white universities in 1965–66, the academic world itself scarcely noticed Blacks. Scholars like Professor Melville Herskovits of Northwestern and psychologists like Klineberg sought to disprove the all-pervasive myth of Black mental inferiority, but the university had not exerted itself as an institution to create positive solutions to the racial caste system. Therefore, it had no claim to be either better or worse than the rest of American society when the years of reckoning from 1967 to 1971 arrived. The university fancied itself free of racism and imbued with the belief that it is the man, not the color, that counts. But self-perception is often fatally in conflict with the perception of others. The white American university, as viewed by Blacks, was white and racist.

4

Power to the People

Racial Strife on the Campuses, 1965-71

White America's colleges had little notion of the conflict and turmoil that would cripple some of them when they first began, in the mid-sixties, to accept "underprepared" Black students into the freshman courses. The first steps of these small groups of Black students onto their campuses were like the first probing artillery rounds onto the territory of a hitherto neutral power. Historically uncaring about the fate of Black people, the university was ill-prepared to face the three hundred years of pent-up feeling that the students brought with them to the campus. And one can make little sense of the actions and attitudes of Black students as they entered colleges over the past five years without a clear understanding of the forces being exerted upon them by the outside world.

The past ten years have been the most tumultuous period in Black American life since Reconstruction. The central thrust of the Black movement was the assertion by Afro-Americans of their right to the same economic, social, and political benefits enjoyed by the majority of white Americans. The movement began as an attack on the social and political racism of the American South, and many thought it would come to its climax there. Shifts in society—movements of people, capital, and land ownership—often escape the view of leaders of social change. Prisoners of their own visions of right and wrong, they may fail to see, as the Luddites did, the powerful economic levers of change that will first blunt, then destroy their movement. While Martin Luther King demonstrated and jeopardized his life for the integration of Blacks into the white Southern structure, many Blacks had migrated from the rapidly mechanizing Southern agricultural structure to the urban areas of both the South and North. The center of Black America's struggle came to rest in Bed-Stuy, Watts, Hough, and Rochester.

The shift of Black Americans from rural to urban areas resulted in the development of the so-called central cities and the heavy concentration of Blacks in urban school districts. This changed composition of cities and schools burst upon a Northern white population deeply indoctrinated with racial stereotypes of Black people. One, of course, could draw parallels between any movement from rural to urban areas and detail, in abstract, what would occur even without the incubus of racial stigmas. One would find among rural inhabitants traits ill-suited to survival in an urban environment. They are uniformly less well educated than their urban counterparts, less disciplined to the demands of industrial work, and less able to manipulate the political and social mechanisms already existent in a city. The transition from the country to the town also brings with it a breakup both of the family unit and of the extended clan system that supports the individual in the rural environment. In short, the traditional structure is destroyed and the individual finds nothing with which to replace it. He stands alone in a hostile and seemingly unmanipulable environment. For the newly urbanized Black male, this means presiding over the dissolution of his family and manhood, while unemployment, poor schools, rat-infested housing, and white-controlled narcotics destroy any possibility of a viable home existence. To be sure, not all migrants to the central cities have come directly from Southern rural backgrounds to metropolitan areas. There is evidence that recently half of the migration to cities is interurban, i.e., Blacks moving from one metropolitan area to another. But whether those persons are complete newcomers to an urban area or migrants from another city, their lives in the central cities will be dominated by a struggle for economic and social survival in a white-controlled society.

The combination of the plight of the urban Black and the courage and unifying ability of Martin Luther King, although primarily directed toward the rural Black, led to the concept of "Black Power" in its application to the central cities. One need not agree with King's philosophy of nonviolence nor his inevitably integrationist stand to understand that his movement brought pride and a sense of mission and unity to all strata of Black people. His was the first Black-led, mass political and social movement upon whose principles most Blacks could agree. King's stands in the face of dogs, gas, and bull whips projected a new image of Black strength and unwillingness to accept abjectly the racial status quo.

At the same time, King's philosophy provided a tilting wall for those Blacks who felt that the solution to the Black situation lay in Black self-determination. The Black Muslims antedated the King movement by nearly three decades, but the concept of Black power developed by Stokely Carmichael, Malcolm X, and Floyd McKissick gained strength and credibility among large numbers of Black people precisely because of the inapplicability of King's philosophy to the Black urban masses. These individuals came to embody the intellectual antithesis of the King philosophy. Malcolm's and Stokely's strong image of Black men intolerant of assaults upon their bodies and souls appealed greatly to the Black urban population who understood all too readily that integration was a "mess of pottage." They could not move from their homes, they could not avoid the assaults of policemen, and they had no means of avoiding the intellectual insults daily perpetrated upon their children by white schoolteachers. They were free to vote and free to eat where they would, but prisoners all the same.

The speeches and writings of Malcolm X and Stokely Carmichael began as a stance rather than a rigid ideology, but the thoughts and actions of both directed themselves to the assertion of Blackness. In masterful inversions, they managed to turn the word "Black" into a symbol of pride rather than shame. And from their efforts sprang further examinations into the alternatives open to Black people in this country. They ranged from Yoruba cults to political Pan-Africanism to Pantherism to the reclamation of Southern lands by Blacks for a new Republic of Africa. The progression is found in LeRoi Jones' change from village poet to Imamu Baraka, political and spiritual leader in Newark; from Lew Alcindor to Kareem Jabbar, from Cassius Clay to Muhammad Ali. It is not by chance that all three were among the most privileged in terms of the possibilities open to them to succeed in white America. The reaction to King was further evident in the Afros, dashikis, and the celebration, by some, of those Black "traits" most opposite to those of white America. Supposed vices became virtues—contrasting the easygoing "soulful" nature of Blacks with the rigidity of uptight white suburbanites, or "natural" Black athletic rhythm with the stolid, methodical play of whites. In some cases, that of the Panthers, the return to Blackness evolved into the ideological stance of the Third World movement. In others, for example the case of the Black Muslims, there was an insistence that members, although hating the "white devil," take on the discipline and attention to detail that characterized the "devil." All of this ideological movement took place within a context of fire and blood in the Black enclaves of Watts, Detroit, and Newark. The development of the Black Power movement was the intellectual manifestation of the outrage felt by Black persons trapped on an escalator that seemed to go nowhere.

Major contributors to the intensity of the Black movement of the middle 1960s were the publicist Michael Harrington and the Black academician Kenneth Clark who, in 1954, had been instrumental in obtaining the Supreme Court victory against segregated schools. Harrington's *The Other America* laid bare the conditions of life for poor people in the midst of a supposedly affluent society and was crucial in developing a consensus among the white liberal intelligentsia that a national policy to eliminate poverty was needed. In the meantime, Clark's detailed 1965 study on Harlem, *Dark Ghetto*, preceded by *Youth in the Ghetto* (1964), had concluded that the major cause of the desperate state of ghetto inhabitants was their inability to control or influence any of the state mechanisms that affected their lives. His remedy was to create community-controlled structures as a counterforce to governmental agencies. The concept was given federal recognition through the funding of HarYou Act and the subsequent development of similar "war on poverty" programs throughout the country. Thus, institutionalized mechanisms for organized protests by the Black urban poor were created at exactly the same time that an ideology of Black Power was coming into existence. Clark's emphasis on "powerlessness" was soon supplanted by a sense on the part of the poor and their leaders that the Black community should not only counterpoise the white bureaucracy but indeed wrench the levers of control, be they welfare or housing, from white society and place them under the direction of the populations of the central cities. Indeed, one could well argue that the genesis of the slogan "Power to the People" lay more in the rise of the Black community poverty programs and their commingling with Black Power ideology than with any Third World or Maoist influences. Nevertheless, in the middle sixties, the heroics of Che Guevara, Castro, and the Vietcong, together with the theoretical works of Frantz Fanon, had a substantial impact on the development of the new Black consciousness.

Having lived so recently during these changes, it is difficult to view in perspective what took place. It is obvious that when an oppressed people raise their expectations, a variety of ideologies begin to form. Confronted with constituencies demanding change, some leaders will arise who wish to return to the past, others will draw parallels with successful contemporary revolutionary ventures, and still others will demand minimal concessions from the oppressing system. For our purposes, the intellectual incubator of the Black students now in white colleges was a multiplicity of ideologies and actions all directed toward Black assertiveness.

As we have noted earlier, the colleges that the Black students entered were already in a state of instability. The Vietnam war, the implausible explanations and duplicities of the Johnson Administration, had created tensions among faculty and students that began to shatter the pre-1964 consensus. Robert Nisbet has noted that even prior to the student upheavals there had been a considerable rise in professorial participation in campus affairs: "Faculty preoccupation with academic-political issues . . . in many places [had] become almost incessant." [1] The faculties' self-assertion was soon followed by white students across the country as the S.D.S. or local radical groups began to focus their sights on the university. Typical issues which triggered student uprisings were the submission of male class rankings to draft boards; on-campus recruitment by the CIA, the military, or companies associated with the manufacture of weapons; the presence on campus of the ROTC; links between the university and defense research institutes; and student power over curriculum and personnel matters. At Columbia, the precipitating factor in the April 1968 revolt was the university's affiliation with the Institute of Defense Analysis, a nonprofit, Defense Department-funded research organization designed to develop weaponry administered by a consortium of twelve universities. Stanford, in 1967–68, experienced disruptions related to CIA recruiting on campus, whereas at the University of Chicago a sit-in took place in 1966, protesting the releasing of class rankings to draft boards. Throughout the nation, in the years 1965–68, teach-ins escalated to sit-ins and on to physical attacks against military and industrial recruiters. Deans of students began, not frequently in jest, to refer to their domains as departments of "wildlife control." Collegiate unity had been broken.

In this environment of troubled campuses and a new Black militancy, white colleges throughout the country began actively to recruit Black students. No one seems to have an accurate count of the total number of Black students in white colleges, because of the inadequacies of data collection and the reluctance of many institutions, at least publicly, to identify the student body by race. From available data, however, it is clear that a revolution has been sweeping the nation's colleges in terms of the number of Black students admitted. In 1960, there were 200,000 Black collegians, 65 per cent of whom were enrolled in Black colleges.[2] By 1964, there were 234,000 black collegians, 51 per cent of whom were enrolled in Black colleges. By 1970, the population of Black students had increased to almost 500,-000, only 34 per cent of whom were enrolled in Black institutions. But of the Black students enrolled in white institutions, half were students in two-year community colleges.[3] Perhaps the best estimate would be that the student bodies of two-year colleges had a 7.9 per cent Black enrollment, four-year public colleges 3.1 per cent, and private four-year institutions 2 per cent. The figures should be assessed carefully. Among the four hundred public four-year institutions containing some 122,000 Black students, for example, the City University of New York and its open admissions policy accounts for well over 15 per cent of the national total, with other institutions such as Wayne State in Detroit accounting also for large chunks of the total national picture.[4] The bulk of this increment of Black students in four-year institutions occurred in the years 1967–71.

Typically, the recruitment of Black students began when either the faculty or the administration of a college, responding to increasing Black pressure from the outside, began to examine their consciences. Having done so, they began small pilot efforts, at Harvard in the late fifties for example, to seek out talented Black students from around the country who, although they could not meet traditional Harvard entry requirements, had demonstrated outstanding ability in their environments. A vale-dictorian of an all-Black high school in the South with low Scholastic Aptitude Test scores was considered a likely candidate for Harvard after a year in a prep school or a special summer session. Such sessions also took place at Dartmouth. The same type of experiment occurred at Rutgers in 1965, where a group of faculty members decided to give Black students with good high school averages but low S.A.T.s the opportunity to enter Rutgers under special dispensations. At the City College of New York, in 1964, talks resulted in the admission of students whose high school averages were low but whose transcripts indicated areas of academic strength. All of the programs took note of the financial disabilities of Black students and all promised supplementary academic assistance.

Most white colleges soon encountered a difficulty that ex-acerbated the recruitment problems. They faced the naked fact that most Blacks emerging from high schools, no matter how one looked for potential, were far removed academically from traditional college admission standards. The statistics on the ed-ucational achievement of Black youth are depressingly con-sistent in their findings on the disparity between the academic level of Black and white youth. If one takes the research done by the College Entrance Examination Board, the proportion of

Black high school seniors who would score 400 or above on the verbal section of the Scholastic Aptitude Test is approximately 15 per cent of the total pool of such seniors. Only some 2 per cent of that same pool would score 500 or above on that test of verbal ability. To give some idea of comparable national averages, 45 per cent of all high school seniors score above 400 and 20 per cent above 500 on the same test.[5] The 1966 Coleman report, although heavily criticized for its methodology, haste, and interpretations of data, found that Black students inevitably fell 1.1 standard deviations below the achievement of white students: "At grade 6, this represents 1.6 years behind, at grade 9, 2.4 years, and at grade 12, 3.3 years." [6] Pre-induction tests of draftees in the period 1964–65 gave essentially the same kind of results. Over the total country, 14.5 per cent of whites failed the test, while 59.3 per cent of Blacks failed. Forty-five per cent of the whites fell into the top 35 per cent of those taking the test, while 7.9 per cent of Blacks were in that category.[7] The entire school sequence from elementary school through high school had so failed to educate Black youth that the colleges were forced—frequently prodded by the small cadres of Blacks earlier admitted—to begin searching for Black students who fell into the middle and bottom ranges of their high school classes. The universities were thus brought face to face with urban Black youth who were far removed academically from their traditional Black clientele.

Nothing so clearly illustrates the transition that took place in the years 1965–69 as the Onyx Society at City College. One day, in 1966, a young Black student approached me and diffidently inquired as to whether I would be willing to serve as the faculty adviser to some Black students who had decided to band together as the "Onyx Society." It was a group of comparatively conservative students, all admitted under regular City College standards, and all of whom felt some need to relate to one another socially and to do service in the community. Within a year, the leadership of the society had passed to more militant students—still regularly admitted—who began to draw for membership on the students specially recruited under City College's SEEK program. The assassination of Martin Luther King in 1969 brought into existence an even more militant leadership and increased demands for Black admissions quotas, and by the spring of 1970, the Onyx Society had become almost completely submerged by a radical coalition of special and regularly admitted students who spearheaded the occupation of the campus for three weeks and became the force that led to the open admissions system, now the official policy of the City University of New York.

In the mid-1960s few white institutions had taken positive action toward the elimination of racism, either in the country at large or in the institutions in particular. Few had any Black faculty members, few had been sensitive to the spiritual anguish that afflicted those Black students in the colleges—grateful for the education, but full of grievances that were seldom voiced. These were colleges that accepted with equanimity and a sense of normality such conditions as all-white fraternities, Newman Clubs, Hillel Societies, all-white clerical and administrative staffs, and professors whose sole academic concern was White America. The colleges, moreover, were operating on the premise that they were doing Black students a favor by permitting them to enter their institutions. The sentiment has been voiced to me by dozens of college administrators: "Why do 'they' act this way when we are permitting 'them' entry into the mainstream of American society?" Acting on the assumption that admitting Black students was somewhat akin to divine dispensation, universities felt no particular pressure to make special arrangements for the newcomers. On the other hand, the limited pool of "academically qualified" Black youngsters meant that the colleges increasingly brought onto their campuses Black youth who not only had experienced deprivation and white scorn but were also sensitive to every conscious or unconscious manifestation of racism. The problem lay in the fact that the colleges had failed to do what their professors daily preached to their classes: conceptualize. Thus, with few exceptions, every demand of the Black students burst upon them like a concussion grenade.

If the sheer whiteness of most campuses had not been stimulus enough to explosive action, then the pressures of the outside world and the ideological bent of the Black intelligentsia would have triggered the difficulties experienced on most campuses. Reinforced by the National Guard and police encounters in American ghettos and by police murders of Black protesters like Fred Hampton in Chicago, young Blacks inevitably responded, their racial memories awakened to the present and the past of oppression. Add to these combustible factors many Black students who had neither the academic skills traditionally deemed necessary to finish college nor the pull of their home communities. The militant organizations sometimes went so far as to tell them that they did not belong in college, but instead should be serving as revolutionary soldiers in the communities.[8]

Every one of the dozens of Black student uprisings which occurred during 1967–70, it seems fair to say, had substantive justification; yet, even the demands enunciated in the inevitable confrontations in presidents' conference rooms, extreme as many considered them, did not wholly reflect the students' real grievances and, if accepted, would not have alleviated their anger. The root causes of the hostility which Black students expressed frequently lay deep, in the tumult gripping both Black communities and the campuses.

That basic hostility was reinforced by myriad petty and grand insults paid the Black youth by the university. At Columbia, where Blacks in 1968 occupied a building demanding that the university cease efforts to construct a gymnasium in Harlem, the Cox Commission reported: "At Columbia, the security guards were long allowed to follow the unforgivable practice of inspecting Black students' identification cards when they entered college buildings, although the white students were passed without notice."[9] The famous armed sit-in of Black students at Willard Strait Hall at Cornell began as a direct result of a burning cross tossed onto the porch of a dormitory occupied by young Black women. At San Francisco State, a radical shift in admissions policy distinctly unfavorable to Blacks was the cause of a confrontation. Although the Donahue Higher Education Act of 1960 had provided free access to postsecondary education with the top 12½ per cent of students entering the University of California system, the top third the state colleges, and the remainder into community colleges, San Francisco State in 1965 added as an admissions criterion the S.A.T., thus precipitating an actual drop in the number of Black students on campus between the years 1965 and 1968.

Nor were relations between Black and white students on campuses particularly friendly. In many colleges the S.D.S. supported Black demands, but in almost every case, the Black students refused to permit white radicals to engage in activities initiated by the Blacks. The split was precipitated both by the prevailing Black ideology of "separatism" and by a basic distaste among Black students for the whole life style of the white radical. Even more important, Black demands usually centered on concrete goals such as admission procedures, financial aid, or Black studies, while the white radical demands were diffuse, often directed at matters over which the university had little or no control. A more serious split between white and Black students occurred on campuses where whites were not radicals but simply "typical" American college students. At Northwestern University, for some two years before the April 1968 sit-in by Black students, administration officials report instances of "white students hitting Negro students with full beer cans, white 'goon squads' beating Negro students, and white students attempting to run down Negro students with cars." [10] Black students at Wesleyan University sponsored a "soul" concert by Wilson Pickett in December 1967, during which some whites ". . . shouted, hooted, made lavish use of the word 'nigger' and in a final act of gallantry, took off their pants." [11] At Yale, after the death of Martin Luther King, a white student went over to a breakfasting Black and said, "I was terribly sorry to hear about King's death . . . but I'm interested to know how all this affects a Negro. Would you mind telling me just how you reacted to this?" [12]

Many administrators and professors were little better than the students in their attitudes toward the newly arrived Blacks. Black applicants for assistance were often treated like welfare clients by bursars and financial officers. Most professors, teaching as they had always taught, would inject into discussions their own middle-class bias about poor people, never thinking that the children of those persons sat before them. At Cornell, for example, a visiting professor said that "slum children play sick and perverted games stressing cunning and survival in the jungle." [13] At the City College of New York, a radical professor (a picture of Mao hung in his office) asked all of the special admissions students to stand up and identify themselves to the class. By midterm, all of these students had been failed. Speaking of an orientation session with Black students, one faculty member at Wesleyan said, "The Blacks began by demanding that we accept the proposition that Wesleyan is a racist institution. I told them that was rubbish. If it were a racist institution, they wouldn't be here." [14] He could not understand why the Black students took this statement as an insult. In reply to a survey of attitudes of Black and white professors in integrated institutions, one white professor noted that, "We liberals still feel that we can use the term 'nigger' and laugh at ethnic jokes because we all know we really don't mean it and are not prejudiced. I wonder." [15] Harvard-trained professors would slip into terms such as "You people" and turn to the single Black student in the classroom to explain why Black people acted the way they did. Courses in American literature, even those dealing with minor American figures, would dismiss Richard Wright with contempt. And inevitably—scores of Black students have told this to me—there was a preconception on the part of many white professors that to be Black was to be dumb. This prejudice, felt by earlier generations of Blacks in white colleges, became even more pronounced with the advent of "disadvantaged" Black students onto the campuses.

Like most other white Americans, faculty members were products of a racist society and found it difficult to adjust to the presence of Black faces in their classrooms—particularly when those students, contrary to the liberally acceptable integrationist stance, would appear actively disdainful and skeptical. Issues to which faculties had seldom given much thought—the wage scale of the Black cafeteria workers or the absence of Blacks on university-sponsored construction projects—suddenly became the causes of loud and prolonged confrontations. The demonstrations, frequently led by dashikied Blacks with dark glasses who aroused feelings of fear among the faculty, brought to the surface of their minds the other side of the white stereotype of Black Americans—that of vengeful African "savages."

In short, all the biases that could be found in the white world outside were present, in abundance, within the white academic community. I can scarcely forget a three-hour casual conversation held months before the City College seizure, in which three Black E.O.P. students came in to talk about the things that disturbed them. For a year they had been exposed to a remedial curriculum with highly talented and dedicated Black and white teachers using both white and Black literature as a means of awakening their intellectual potential. Now thrust into the mainstream of the college's curriculum, they found themselves almost daily insulted, ignored, and generally denigrated in their regular courses. The three young men, all of whom had demonstrated academic competence, were among those who began the movement to seize the City College campus. It is small wonder, then, that a survey of Black students at one institution concluded that "the prevailing Black viewpoint is more typical of an exploited colonial people than of an upwardly mobile group." [16]

The storms that ensued across the country, then, were of multiple genesis, but their essence was the same: "If you're going to admit us to the university," Black students were saying, "and are unable to provide the environment in which we, as Black people, can feel human, then we ask the right to create those structures within the university that will enable us to do so."

One need not replicate, college by college, Black students' demands. They are easily summarized:

1. That there be a department of Black studies, with the faculty and chairman elected by the students and Black faculty (in some cases) of the college.

2. That a special quota for Black students be established by the university which, at a minimum, would equal the percentage of Blacks in the population at large.

3. That special dormitory facilities be established for Black students.

4. That a cultural center for Black students be created.

5. That the administration grant a specific number of full,

associate, and assistant professorial lines to the Department or School of Black Studies.

6. That the curriculum developed by Black faculty and students be approved by the college.

7. That special funds be allocated for academic assistance of Black students.

8. That no Black student be expelled for academic reasons for a period of two years.

9. That the chairman of the Department of Black Studies report directly to the president of the university.

10. That the usual criteria for faculty recruitment be waived in the case of Black faculty members.

11. That Black students involved in this action receive amnesty from criminal and academic sanctions.

12. That Black students receive passing grades if they were involved in this political action.

13. That Black students be permitted to receive credit for work done in the community.

14. That Black faculty and students have veto power over the hiring of any Black faculty and administrators in the college.

15. That Black counselors be hired who can relate to the real needs of Black students.

These demands, usually delivered in strident voice with an accompaniment of choice Black invective, exploded upon administrator after administrator throughout the country. They were astounded by the demands and the rage. After all, hadn't they served on the boards of the NAACP, hadn't they marched to Selma, hadn't they invited Bayard Rustin to lecture at the campus? In short, what had they done to deserve these verbal and sometimes physical assaults in the name of demands for Black autonomy?

In the course of political and social analysis, it does not always make sense to quantify a problem. In this particular instance, white administrators would have been far better prepared for what awaited them with the entrance onto the campuses of Black students had they long beforehand immersed themselves in the study of Black literature. For the Black students' demands—often from fewer than 50 people on a campus of 10,000—carried with them the weight of every slight and injury suffered by Africans from the time they were stolen from their ancestral villages. The incoherence of some of the demands was a reflection of rage and of contempt.

What justification can there be for the "outrageous" categorization of demands listed above? The demands—as they were put by Blacks—can be generally categorized into four types: first, the demand for a Black-controlled Black studies enclave; second, the demand for dormitory and cultural space for Black students; third, the demand for additional admissions quotas for Black students; fourth, the demand that Black students be given special tutorial and financial aid, and academic dispensations.

Absolutely none of these demands should be intolerable or incomprehensible to any university cognizant of its own past history. The first demand, that of a Black studies department run by Black people, is in the intellectual tradition of Du Bois, Carter Woodson, and other Black scholars who felt that the study of Black people should primarily be the concern of Black scholars. Both the past and present writings of most white scholars on Black matters give little indication that Du Bois was wrong on this point. Within the context of a white-dominated institution, Black students were naturally well aware that deans of administration, personnel and budget committees, and the general faculty would be ill-disposed toward a Black-controlled department: therefore, the demand for autonomy of such a department and the guaranteeing of adequate staffing and funding. Knowing the power of curriculum committees, it is also obvious that Black students and faculty would demand that their course offerings not be subject to the approval of a conservative body that would have instinctive doubts on whether the field of Black studies constituted, in fact, a legitimate subject of academic concern. The second demand, that of a place where Blacks could be together, seems too well justified to even contest. If university administrations have tolerated for one hundred years exclusive groupings of students masked under the names of societies, fraternities, or clubs, but all the same exclusionary, why should the rules suddenly be changed when a group of Black students, historically rejected by those university-sanctioned enclaves, asks for the same privilege? Third, if the universities, by virtue of standards frequently waived for athletes and sons of alumni, have been historically content with a minuscule number of Black students on their campuses, do they not have a duty to redress that historical imbalance? And why, if the liberal conscience exists, need Black students face jail terms to force the universities to do what the universities should have done long ago? The fourth and last category of demand is directed to the influx into white institutions of students ill-prepared both intellectually and financially to complete a four-year institution. It simply states that an educational imbalance built upon a long history of injustice cannot easily be destroyed. Peripheral attention to students who enter the university suffering the consequences of that injustice will not redress that imbalance.

These rationales for the actions of Black students should not be interpreted as an uncritical acceptance of all the noise, fury, and rhetoric that accompanied the Black student movement of the past four years. Just as white universities failed to anticipate the impact of the Black influx onto their campuses, so had Black intellectuals and Black students failed to conceptualize exactly what was wanted from the white universities into which they were entering. There was a distinct failure, understandable in the midst of rapid changes of ideology, to crystallize an all-embracing and realistic strategy for deriving the best things for Black people from this suddenly opened door. Behind the concreteness of demands—some clearly logical, some apparently absurd—lay a deeper, inarticulated demand: to be taken seriously as human beings and to be treated as any respected human being would be treated.

In short, no one had created a blueprint that began with the needs of the Black urban masses and moved from that condition to a serious appraisal of the way in which the lives of Black people could be improved by the entrance of Afro-American students into previously all-white colleges. The words "liberation," "self-determination," and "nation-building" were used interminably by all varieties of Black political thinkers, but there was no common definition of those phrases besides getting the white man's boot off of Black necks.

The most devastating impact of white racism is its encourage-
ment of a lack of intellectual discipline among Black youth. The
figures on Black achievement in standard tests are eloquent wit-
ness to the failure of public schools to teach Black children to
read and write. This is a consequence of white society's stereotype—present in the most enlightened circles—of the Black man
as lazy, incapable of learning, unpunctual, and devoid of the
concentration span necessary to develop conceptual skills. Until
recently, nothing in the training of teachers prepared them to
believe otherwise. The entire educational process for teachers
was premised on the fact that they would find in their classrooms carbon copies of themselves.[17] The curriculum that most
would-be teachers must follow, heavily determined by a matrix
of teachers' unions, state education departments, professors of
education, and the NEA,[18] is a potpourri of foundations of education, educational psychology, and methodology courses that do
little to prepare them for the type of student they will meet in
all-Black elementary or high schools. The curricula that the
teachers must follow for both elementary and secondary students are themselves tightly bound by accrediting and local
school board restrictions. The result appears meaningless to
many poor Black students. There is little in the traditional liberal arts–education major curriculum that deals with Black people. One former Harvard education student said that: "As to
my own experiences and reactions to Harlem teaching, let me
say that I was initially totally unprepared and totally at a loss
. . . Harvard's assumptions, methods, and approaches simply did
not prepare me at all, and are totally irrelevant to the lower
class urban Negro children I'm now teaching." [19]

The newly graduated teachers are thus thrust into ghetto
schools completely unequipped to teach the Black faces in front
of them. Once in the schools, even if possessed of a *mission civil-
isatrice,* they find themselves frustrated: "Using the traditional
tools and techniques, he fights a losing battle. He struggles to put
across a concept, an attitude, and finds the next day he has accomplished nothing. He too accepts the situation and decides
that the pupils are uneducable.[20]

If the failure of the children to respond to a textbook full of
allusions to summer vacations on lovely beaches does not con-

vince the teacher of the innate mental inferiority of Black children, then some experienced white colleague will do so. The superintendent of schools in Syracuse in 1967 told the U.S. Commission on Civil Rights that teachers in Black schools tend "to average down" their expectations of academic achievement from the students.[21] So almost from the moment a Black child enters into most white teachers' kindergarten classes—and this is further documented in the works of James Herndon, James Haskins, and Jonathan Kozol—the youngster is expected to conform to an inferior stereotype. Thus begins a deadly cycle. The children understand quickly that little is demanded of them and they, in turn, begin to conform to the expected. Teachers, from the elementary school up, feel that they have turned in a good day's work if they manage to have no physical disruptions in their classes. By the time Black children enter into junior and senior high schools, usually staffed predominantly by white teachers and supervisors, the self-fulfilling prophecy is well on its way to realization. Students walk freely through the halls, the principal is happy if he has 40 per cent attendance, academic standards are tossed aside, learning ceases to exist, and students are permitted to graduate with reading, writing, and math skills approximating those of a sixth- to eighth-grader in a white suburban school system. The Black student has, in fact, become intellectually undisciplined, incapable of sustained attention to a complex science textbook, and unable to perform well on any of the standard measuring instruments of academic proficiency.

Does total blame rest on the shoulders of the schoolteachers? No, for there are other inputs into the development of these youth, and for the most part, they are antithetical to the growth of their intellectual potential. The marginal economic state of most ghetto families and their sense—rooted in the realities of job opportunities for Blacks—that even an educated Black will be denied an equal chance in this society, initially discourage a Black youth's ambitions. Moreover, the student will be faced with a paucity of space for study, crowded living conditions, and brothers and sisters to whom he must act as a babysitter. The student's health may be poor and yet medically undiagnosed. Finally, the Black adolescent, although Black, is an adolescent, with all that suggests in terms of seeking an adult identity. By the time the youth turns sixteen, powerful emotional and cultural pulls begin to turn him away from an educational system that, in itself, has already shown little holding power. The family's financial plight may mean that the adolescent feels it is time to become a man and contribute money to the family. Moreover, the Black urban youth, like any American teen-ager, is subjected daily to invitations to the good life—that of cars, stereos, and fine clothes. Without parents who can give him these things, and surrounded by street people who, despite their lack of education, have managed to display conspicuous financial success through various activities, the pull of the streets and its world of hustlers becomes powerful indeed. It is no coincidence that the highest dropout rate for Black students in New York City's high schools occurs in the junior year of high school. Racism has its impact on Black youth, then, not only in the non-education they receive, but also in every other aspect of their daily lives. Nothing has prepared them for the academic demands, the rigor of thought and concentration, that await them on the campus where they have been accepted as special-admissions students.

The Black student being admitted to a white college must of necessity undergo a 180-degree turn. This transformation is made even more difficult by the romanticized Black street life of pimps, numbers writers, and "hustlers" depicted by some Black contemporary writers, poets, and movies. One cannot have it both ways: if the caste system in this country is harmful to Black people, then one cannot escape the conclusion that many of the traits deemed "Black" are nothing more than manifestations of the spiritual, social, and economic oppression wrought upon Black people by white society over three centuries. Put another way, if the academic deficiencies of Black students are due to environmental causes, then there are a multiplicity of factors in that environment that hinder educational achievement, just as there are strengths built into them by their sheer ability to survive. Of the negative traits, the most intellectually devastating is that of "spontaneity"—do your own thing—encouraged by both the white educational establishment and some of the new school of Black writers. In effect, the high school student is being told that nobody cares what happens to him in terms of his being equipped with the academic skills necessary to survival in the modern world. It is interesting to note that the traits so often ascribed to Blacks are precisely those associated with peasant and poverty cultures throughout the world. One could read mid-nineteenth-century descriptions of the European peasantry that duplicate, almost word for word, present-day celebrations of spontaneity and naturalness.

Yet, the history of Russia's, Germany's, and Britain's industrialization indicates that the creation of technological power means the devaluation of traits traditionally attributed to peasant and newly urbanized cultures. The large-scale building of armies, factories, bridges, and power plants depends upon a people rooted in habits of punctuality, attention to detail, and long-term concentration on the problem at hand. Black educators must understand that no matter what the political end, it can only be accomplished by instilling disciplined academic habits of work into Black youth. These have nothing to do with "Whitey's" values or the Protestant Ethic, but are, in fact, the same values that Castro, Mao, Nasser, and Nyere have attempted to inject into their peasant cultures in order to attain a state of political and economic autonomy vis-à-vis the West. And in the process of the transformation of Black youth, it is certain that many of those traits traditionally associated with Blackness will be modified in accordance with new priorities.

Does this mean, then, that an ideology of Blackness and a sense of Black unity have no part in the education of Black youth? Of course not, since it is within the context of this ideology and motivation that Black educators can focus on the real problems of Black students—their lack of math, reading and writing skills, and the white-induced lack of intellectual discipline. Whether the aim be the creation of a cohesive Pan-African movement, a Black enclave within the United States, or economic and political (if not social) integration into America, it is necesary to instill this discipline. The success of the Black Muslims' educational system is ample testimony to the way in which ideology and learning can be mated.

The major critique to be made of the "demands" of Black students is that they were devoid, for the most part, of demands that the colleges give them the academic support necessary to break the white stranglehold on those disciplines centered around mathematics. It makes far better sense that the students demand a ten-hour-per-week college math preparatory course than that they demand that no Black student should be flunked out of college for two years. In the same way, the demands, for the most part, were devoid of requests that the universities provide 10 per cent of their graduate school openings to Black students, or of demands that Black administrators and professors be recruited on a quota basis for the regular academic departments of the colleges. As a result, most colleges have been able to "fulfill" their obligations to the Black community by the creation of enclaves of Black studies programs and Black E.O.P. programs, usually topped by a Black administrator called "coordinator," "vice-chancellor," "special assistant to the chancellor" of community or minority affairs.

The explosion in the Black student population in white colleges over the past five years was a phenomenon for which neither the colleges nor Black intellectuals were prepared. The result has been a chaotic and somewhat nonproductive epoch in the higher education of Black students. The white colleges received a population with whom they had no previous experience, expected that the mere act of admission would show their goodwill, and made efforts to carry on business as usual. On the other hand, within the Black community, beyond vague thoughts about the racism of whites, there had been little attempt to develop the details of a Black educational plan that looked beyond the concession by the colleges of the need for a Black studies program, and asked "What do we want for our children, given the hard fact that they will be educated within the context of a white educational environment?"

5

Bridging the Gap

Compensatory Education Programs in White Colleges

The entrance of Black students onto predominantly white campuses posed a direct threat to the basic value systems of the universities. The university viewed itself, despite a multiplicity of relationships with industry and government, as a "collection of books and scholars" devoted to an unswerving search for truth and knowledge. The Berkeley revolt signaled the beginning of the end of this traditional view and resulted in some cracks in the ivory tower. Still unchallenged in the minds of many faculty and administrators, however, were certain premises upon whose continued existence they felt the very fate of the university hinged. The first was that a combination of high school averages and college entrance examination scores provided the best basis for evaluating a student's potential for academic success in a particular institution of higher learning. Of course, certain other factors, such as athletic participation, leadership in high school government, or outstanding achievement in some particular area of scholarship, might compensate to a slight degree for a student's weaknesses in tests and grades, but all in all, the scholastic aptitude tests and the high school averages were accurate guides as to whether a student would succeed in college or not. And indeed, that was true: the belief in tests and grades was a self-fulfilling prophecy. The "best" students went to Harvard, Berkeley, Swarthmore, Vassar, and the University of Michigan, and graduated from these institutions to achieve great success in later life. The "best" faculty taught at these places, and one could measure the prestige of an academic appointment by correlating it with the average S.A.T.s of the entering freshman class. Professorial status was, and is, directly linked to admission criteria.

A second major premise of most academicians was a belief in the sanctity of standards. Thus, a student's proficiency in passing through the 120 credits of course work with an A-average was greatly admired and rewarded with a Phi Beta Kappa key and fellowships to graduate schools. However, a student who fell below the college's requirements would be asked to leave, even at the end of his first semester, because he was not of college caliber. The guardians of the standards were the faculty of the institution, and seldom did they fail to exercise their responsibility for quality control.

It must be remembered, moreover, that in the days before student rebellions, many professors expected nothing but respect for their scholarly wisdom, preferably duly recorded on the midsemester and final examinations. The universities in which the professors worked were stable institutions with a well-established matrix of internal checks and balances. Scholarship was guaranteed to remain the core of the institution, and academic change would only come about after judicious appraisal and due approval by the faculty of its impact on the college. Initial appointments to the faculty, tenure, and promotions were closely guarded prerogatives of the academic departments, and each of these judgments was made, in theory, only after meticulous screening of candidates and of their potential for contributions to the academic life of the institution. The system was highly protective of faculty rights and prerogatives, weighted toward the maintenance of the status quo, and incapable of rapid change. Certain issues—the Vietnam war, the related matters of the draft, military and industrial recruiting on campus—scarcely touched the basic interests of the faculty. One could teach his classes, participate in sit-ins or picketing if he so desired, and still feel no doubts about the quality of the school, his own academic status, and his ability to choose his colleagues and control curricular matters in such a fashion that students would receive a good education.

Admission of Black students into the university, however, and questions of academic changes made necessary by those admissions, struck at the very heart of the faculty member's interests. As pointed out earlier, the number of Black students qualified for admission to white colleges under traditional criteria is small. Thus, the admission of large numbers of Black students to most institutions meant a lowering of entrance requirements and posed a threat both to the status of professors and to the academic "quality" of the colleges. A survey of college professors, with 60,000 respondents, conducted by Professor Martin A. Trow of the University of California at Berkeley, determined that less than half of faculty members "felt that more minority students should be admitted even if it means relaxing admission standards." [1] Moreover, if a college admitted "marginal" students, it had to take some measures to ensure their academic success. These measures and their effects almost invariably touched on the very interstices of academia, for they implied some changes in academic procedures, ranging from the provision of special courses and faculty for such students to changes in retention standards.

In the face of the threats to academia implicit in the admission of Black students, it was inevitable that a faculty backlash would develop even before the number of such students on their campuses became substantial. The most powerful political voice to be raised against special enrollment policies was that of Spiro Agnew, who argued that the merit system of admission to higher education had served all kinds of Americans well, and that it would be a disservice to Blacks were they to be admitted to universities on any basis other than one of true achievement.[2] He found, of course, strong support in academic circles. In the 1969 annual president's address to the American Council on Education, Logan Wilson contrasted the "egalitarian" system of admission to institutions of higher education and the "meritocratic" system of admission. The weight of his speech was on the side of "Meritocracy":

Impacts of the educational process are judged most immediately, of course, by fairly standardized procedures of testing, grading, and certifying. Although these routinized tests of human worth have long been criticized, it has been generally conceded that in an open society evaluation of individuals based primarily on what they know and can do is more equitable and certainly more functional than assigning status according to "who they are." In sum, whatever its defects, the meritocratic principle in higher education does have the virtue of emphasizing *achieved* rather than *ascribed* status.[3]

After suitable pondering on the dilemma posed for the university by claims of the "egalitarians," he suggested an alternative that the Black community had heard one hundred years before: "On the contrary, I believe that we should make more post-secondary options available—including those of a notably vocational emphasis—to the growing number and variety of students. . . . Some form of post-secondary education should be available for everybody, but it is time to emphasize what traditional higher education can and cannot do for the society that supports it."[4]

Amitai Etzioni, chairman of the sociology department at Columbia, deviating from his position of leadership in the academic community's agitation against the war in Vietnam, suddenly became an expert on the education of Black youth in an article in the *Wall Street Journal* (March 17, 1970) entitled "The High-Schoolization of College."[5] He argued that academic standards were now under assault from masses of inferior students and that the "hope that 'compensatory education' will help less prepared whites or blacks to catch up and thus maintain the quality of college is a vain one." He suggested that the solution lay in open admissions of all students in two-year colleges: "If we can no longer keep the floodgates closed at the admissions office, it at least seems wise to channel the general flow away from four-year colleges and towards two-year extensions of high school in the junior and community colleges."

Further evidence of the academic counterattack can be seen in a paper by A. J. Jaffe, who argues that "Further 'openness' can be achieved by still further lowering of admission requirements—indeed they could be abolished altogether—reducing the requirements for a degree, and introducing a 'fail-safe' curriculum." [6]

More scholarly, and hence potentially more convincing, arguments against the admission of underprepared Black students to white four-year colleges came from two sources: one, presumably disinterested; the other, somewhat interested, since one of the authors was formerly on the staff of the Educational Testing Service, and the other is presently the director of its southeastern office. Both arguments attempt to prove the validity of college entrance examinations for predicting the success of Black students. The first source, Professor Julian C. Stanley, declared—with copious references to his own work and, of course, a reference to Arthur R. Jensen—that to place Black students into colleges where tests indicate they would not do well was to put an impossible handicap upon those students.[7] He further suggested that the demand for Black studies emerged out of an understanding on the part of Black students that they could not compete academically with their white peers in regular college courses. After fourteen pages of academic citations, Professor Stanley suddenly astounds the reader, however, by admitting that he has no hard data on the performance of Black students enrolled in college compensatory programs.[8] He expresses a hope that the College Entrance Examination Board will make a study of this matter, but in the meantime *he* is certain that a combination of high school grades and tests predicts the level of college performance for Blacks as well as whites. The second source, "Is the S.A.T. Biased Against Black Students?" by Junius A. Davis and George Temp, in the Fall 1971 issue of the *College Board Review*, is a more tempered argument for the validity of the Scholastic Aptitude Test based on a limited sample of white colleges with Black students. The authors bring into question the results of their study when they indicate that they only established correlations between first-term or first-year college performance and the S.A.T. Persons more familiar with compensatory education programs, though, understand that it is precisely during the first year that Black students have the most difficulty in adjusting to the new white academic environments.

The most widely circulated attack on special admissions programs is also the most devastating—because its author was a "qualified" Black professor. It was made by Thomas Sowell, an associate professor of economics at UCLA, in the *New York Times Magazine* of December 13, 1970. Sowell attempted to make a case against admission of "unqualified" Black students by declaring that some ten thousand "qualified" Black students either did not attend college or attended "the lowest level of Southern Negro colleges" because their places were taken by hopelessly underprepared Black students. It was not by chance that Sowell omitted two important statistics: (1) two million freshmen enter college each year; (2) the proportion of full-time Black students in predominantly white colleges is only 2 per cent, despite the expansion over the past three years of educational opportunity programs. Thus, even if Sowell's ten thousand students had been admitted to white universities, one would still have been left with a situation of de facto segregation in most white institutions.

Thus, the real target of Sowell's article was "underprepared Black students who are in over their heads academically," "inept Black students," and "sickening nests of opportunists and bush-league messiahs." Like Professor Stanley, Sowell believes in the correlation between S.A.T. scores and college performance; and like Stanley, he admits at the end of his essay that he has absolutely no data to support his contentions about the ineffectiveness of E.O.P. programs. Sowell filled his article, however, with anecdotal references to Black demagoguery, gift grades, and "intimidation and physical assaults," thus getting to the guts of the matter as far as white academics were concerned.

Sowell continued his attack on Black students in a book published in 1972.[9] He begins to give clues as to the reasons for his elitist stance as he recites the story of his own upbringing. The emphasis throughout the autobiographical section of the book is on his *own* ability, despite growing up under adverse economic and social conditions, to be highly successful in most academic situations—to the extent that he graduated from Harvard *magna cum laude* and frequently had the highest grade in his class.[10] He specifically says that "it would be unwarranted to draw Horatio Alger conclusions" [11] from his success story, but that is exactly what he does. A second theme throughout the book is a fanatical attachment to standards. Sowell is more Harvard than Harvard. He found that the students at Cornell, Douglass College, and, of course, Howard did not meet his standards of excellence, despite the fact that he acknowledges Cornell drew its students from among the top one per cent of high school graduates in the country.

Sowell has the virtue of consistency. If white students were unable to reach the level of intellectual achievement demanded by him, then it is obvious that Black students on such campuses, entering with below average S.A.T. and high school grades, would be the objects of his scorn. Thus, he states that Cornell's Black students went in over their heads when they were admitted, and that most E.O.P. programs are a "search for misfits." [12] Of compensatory programs in general, Sowell declares that "so many underqualified and sometimes semi-literate Blacks have been hired for such jobs as to create an unacceptable stereotype which the capable man shuns." [13] Of Black students, he states, "I must confess that there are times when I wish a minimum quota could be established for the number of Black students to be found studying in libraries; by the usual standards of body counts, libraries would have to be declared the most 'racist' institutions on many campuses." [14]

What, the puzzled reader asks, is Sowell after? The answer is that he still feels that "underqualified" Blacks have prevented "qualified" Black students from entering the colleges. Sowell, formerly a professor at Cornell, had only to look under his own nose to see the fallacy of this generalization. For those same Black Cornell students that he categorized as "being over their heads" were in fact among the top 2 per cent of Black students across the country in terms of their S.A.T. aptitude scores, the mean of which was 530 to 570.[15] Sowell rests his argument solely on figures from one study and *extrapolates* from that study, which itself noted the wide education disparities among Blacks and whites, to support his thesis.[16] One can only be confounded by this scholar with his emphasis on "standards," ignoring all the literature that flatly contradicts his contentions. For example, in order to support a non sequitur he cites facts from a Ford Foundation study—i.e., that high school counseling for Black students is inadequate—and at the same time ignores the same study's major findings that:

1. If a moderately selective university were to take all of its students from approximately the top one-sixth of the ability spectrum, its "talent pool" would include only 2.5% (34 out of 1383) from minority groups.[17]

The study concludes that this problem "underscores the difficulty of achieving equitable representation for minorities in higher education if any of the conventional rank-ordered tests of academic ability are employed."[18] Thus, Sowell avoids any data that would tend to weaken his argument. It is apparent that he is setting up a straw man as a means of camouflaging his assault upon poor Blacks who have not had the luck to achieve his status in life.

From this statistically shaky base, Sowell concludes that the problem lies in the recruitment and selection of Black students, but nowhere does he blame the compensatory educational structures created by colleges as the primary reason for the large dropout rate in some E.O.P. programs. And even if one takes the case of Cornell, where 50 per cent of such students received academic warnings, is it not miraculous that 50 per cent are succeeding when the mean of their S.A.T. scores was 100 points below that of the regularly admitted Cornell students? Only 50 per cent of *all* entering freshmen in the country complete college.

Sowell's lack of originality appears in both his analyses and his solutions. Stanley, discussing test scores and their relationship to college grades, states: "Suppose that a short ninth grader aproaches the basketball coach and says . . . 'I know that I'm not as tall as any player on the high school team, but you must make special allowances for me because I never had the opportunity to reach my full height potential. . . .' The coach might reply: 'You aren't tall enough to play basketball on this team. . . . I doubt that you can compete with those fellows at your present height. . . . Also, I have little confidence that at your age we can increase your height greatly.' "[19]

Sowell, discussing the same problem: "One could show that height had no effect on the ability to play basketball by showing that 6 foot 10 inch players do practically as well as 7 foot players. . . . But no basketball recruiter would dream of becoming indifferent as between seven-footers and men of average height, much less consider putting midgets on the court." [20]

Sowell's solution to the problems is the creation of preparatory centers for Black students, a plan similar to that of Vice President Agnew;[21] and, like Agnew, Sowell devotes pages to the success story of Dunbar High School in Washington, which twenty-four years ago was an elitist institution, allowing upward mobility for basically middle-class Blacks.[22] To a person with such an elitist viewpoint, Black colleges, quota systems, community control, etc., become objects of wrath.[23]

It would be inappropriate to terminate this discussion of the academic onslaught against the admission of underprepared Black students without examining briefly the work of Arthur R. Jensen, which underpins, in subtle fashion, much of the present-day controversy over Black mental capacity.[24] The thrust of Jensen's thought is this: " 'In the actual race of life . . . the chief determining factor is heredity,' so said Edward L. Thorndike in 1905. Since then the preponderance of evidence has proved him right, certainly as concerns those aspects of life in which intelligence plays a great part." [25]

The general public has taken Jensen's words to mean that Black Americans are genetically inferior in mental capacity to whites. Yet Jensen's article itself is so full of contradictions as to make such a conclusion ludicrous. He begins deviating from his assertion that heredity is all-important when he indicates he can find no strong correlation between scholastic achievement and the "heritability of intelligence." [26] He further weakens his argument when he states that "many other traits, habits, attitudes, and values enter into a child's performance in school besides just his intelligence, and those non-cognitive factors are largely environmentally determined, mainly through influences within the child's family." [27]

Furthermore, Jensen declares that I.Q.s can be boosted as much as 20 to 30 points and "in certain extreme cases as much as 60 or 70 points" by a changed environment. Indeed, according to Jensen, there was a 20-point I.Q. difference between "South African colored children" who were extremely undernourished and those who were well fed in infancy.[28] In the face of massive evidence of malnutrition among Black American babies, though, Jensen argues that "gross nutritional deprivation is rare in the United States." Jensen then alludes to studies that indicate that Black Americans, no matter what their social and economic status, have lower I.Q.s than whites, Indians, or Asians. Unfortunately, he cannot exactly measure the environmental factors in which a child is raised. Finally, giving away the whole game, he indicates that: "The fact that a reasonable hypothesis has not been rigorously proved does not mean that it should be summarily dismissed. . . . I believe such definitive research is entirely possible, but has not yet been done." [29] Jensen appears finally to suggest that the mental ability of Blacks is simply inferior to whites', but he has no proof of this claim.

In the years 1966–70, Educational Opportunity Programs (E.O.P.) began to appear on campuses throughout the country. Institutions as diverse as Wesleyan University, Southern Illinois University, and Rutgers, prodded by the availability of federal funding for such programs, moved belatedly to redress the racial imbalances of their student bodies. There was a wide academic range in the type of student recruited for these colleges, from Black students at Cornell, who, although they fell below the college's usual 660–703 on the verbal S.A.T., were still in the 530–570 range, well above the national average, to students at Rutgers University, where many were chosen from the bottom halves of their high school classes. The City University E.O.P. program randomly selected students over the entire scale from 70 to 80 high school averages, the normal cut-off point for admission to senior colleges.

The question of the treatment of the underprepared Black students who entered the colleges via E.O.P. programs was a matter of great concern to both faculty and administrators. The first and most important consideration was to determine the degree to which such students should be treated as "special." Should the college design a complete remedial structure with courses in English, reading, mathematics, and an introduction to the social sciences? If so, would this not lead to a segregated Black program, and ultimately to the creation of a two-track system within the college? If this course were followed, moreover, should the college grant credit for work of a remedial nature? Or, would it not be wiser for the college and less demoralizing for Black students were they to be placed in a special·summer preparatory session, at the completion of which they would enter directly into the full college freshman curriculum? Maybe, some administrators thought, the best solution was to plunge the students directly into regular college work and provide intensive tutoring on the side, thus obviating the need for marking Black students as "second-class" citizens on campus.

Cutting across all these variations of compensatory education programs was the problem of how much academic leniency was to be granted to specially admitted students. Were retention standards to be altered because such students needed time to repair the gaps in their academic skills, or would not such a policy constitute both "reverse racism" and a dilution of the educational quality of the institution?

If a college decided to create a separate academic structure to house remedial programs, the problems became even more complex. Who was to control the college preparatory curriculum, a special department or the academic departments under whose subject matter the courses fell? And should that compensatory curriculum simply duplicate the content of regular courses, but more slowly, or should it be directly relevant to the life experiences of Black students, and move from that point to more traditional subject matter. Further questions arose about the type of person who should teach the college preparatory courses. Should they be members of the regular faculty, who traditionally have abhorred the concept of teaching "high school" courses, or should they be persons specifically selected for their ability to relate to Black students? If the colleges chose to hire special instructors for E.O.P. programs, then the related question arose as to whether they should be under the jurisdiction—and hence the tenuring and promotion powers—of the college preparatory department or a regular academic department. And, inevitably, conflict erupted around the question of the academic credentials of specially recruited faculty. Should the college waive its regular procedures and grant such faculty instructional titles, or should they instead be given some title that indicated they were not qualified for appointment to the regular staff, but were qualified to teach "remedial" subjects to Black students?

Practically every college ultimately recognized the need for special counseling assistance for Black E.O.P. students. But on that point, too, there was great uncertainty and ambivalence among college administrators. Some chose to hire clinical psychologists, others Black social workers, and still others, under the illusion that Black urban students were best counseled by persons who were close to the streets, hired paraprofessionals. Once they were hired, debates arose as to the role of the counselors. Should they primarily concentrate on psychological therapy, or should they depart from tradition and attempt to deal with all aspects of the student's life that impinged on his academic work?

It is fair to state that no one had the answers to the questions posed above, but as educational opportunities programs began, it was evident that many of them were not constructed so as to give the entering Black students a fair chance at academic success. While some of the blame falls justifiably on the shoulders of the Black directors of such programs and on their staffs, the major share of the blame rests with both the attitudes and practices of white faculty and administrators. At most colleges, the fear of dilution of the academic quality of the institution was of such intensity that it quickly became evident to Black students and the specially recruited Black faculty that they were unwelcome guests, that the colleges were waiting for them to fail, and that the college would take every step necessary to see that a failure occurred.

These attitudes manifested themselves in many ways. Some colleges created six-week compensatory summer curricula and then insisted that the Black students take a full load of college courses. There was an assumption on the college's part that a six-week blitz course could wipe away seventeen years of academic deprivation. Predictably, students in such programs had accumulated so many failing grades by the end of the year that their chances of finishing college were nil. At other institutions, no sequenced structure of college preparatory courses was instituted, but instead the students—some with ninth- and tenth-grade reading levels—were placed into regular courses such as

Economics I, History I, and Chemistry I, and given tutorial assistance. It was obvious that no amount of tutoring would result in the students reading at the expected rate of eight hundred pages a week. In some colleges, Black students entering with major gaps in high school mathematics courses were bluntly told that they would have to take an entire three-year noncredit sequence of such courses before being given matriculated status.

Where colleges moved to create special programs or departments of compensatory education, the attitude of faculties and administrators was even more apparent. Frequently, the physical site of such a program would be in a basement, a temporary building, or, preferably, off-campus. Neither its Black director nor his staff would be given an academic rank, but instead would be designated with some appellation such as "adjunct lecturer." The regular academic departments would either refuse to appoint compensatory education instructors to their staffs, or insist that they possess a Ph.D. degree—even if they had, as in some instances, published five books. Any course deemed by the faculties "remedial" would be denied credit, despite the fact that the reading list in the course might contain titles such as Plato's *Republic* or Camus's *The Rebel*. The net outcome of many compensatory programs was the creation of a class of "Black faculty" with tenuous positions in the colleges, cut off from promotional opportunities and stamped with titles that labeled them as "nonpersons" in the college hierarchy.

The general tendency of the faculties of the English and mathematics departments was to consider themselves too intellectually elevated to participate in the teaching of "remedial subjects" when, after all, they were really specialists in Chaucer or advanced calculus. Faculties, however, were all too ready to give attention to the programs when it came to the question of dropping Black students for reasons of academic failure. No matter that a student with a 65 high school average had progressed from a D— average to one of C— by the end of the year, he still had to be dropped because he had failed to meet the college's traditional academic requirements. Predictably, the manifest racist attitudes and practices of many colleges toward E.O.P. programs produced situations of instability and, sometimes, chaos within the programs. The Black directors, of necessity, were frequently so embroiled in conflicts with college administrators, departmental chairmen, and various faculty committees that they had little time left to devote to the educational task assigned to them by the college. The tenuousness of the positions of directors, staffs, and students produced anxieties throughout many programs that made proper academic planning difficult. In reaction to the onslaught from academia, many E.O.P. programs were transformed into overly protective and politicized strongholds rather than educational launching pads for the gradual movement of the students into the regular college curriculum. Given the environment of many white colleges, it was inevitable that this development would take place, for white faculties and administrators, like mules, had to be hit to get their attention. In short, it was impossible for the programs to function academically until the colleges had been convinced, through one means or another, that underprepared Black students needed special and dedicated attention from the institutions and that neither the students nor the faculty that gave them academic support would tolerate "second-class" status.

When hard data does emerge on the success of E.O.P. programs, it is likely that it will not reflect on the ability of Black students to graduate from white colleges, but on the degree to which a college decided to commit itself, its faculty, and its resources to the task of giving underprepared Black students a fair chance to develop their academic potential. Critics, such as Sowell, Stanley, and Etzioni, may indeed find in the data support for their contention that test scores and high school averages predict college success. But there will be little attention paid to the campus environments in which these programs were spawned, nor will allowances be made for mistakes implicit in any new experiment. "Meritocracy," the College Entrance Examination Board, and the Educational Testing Service will be vindicated.

Yet given the overwhelming social and political pressures that led to special admissions programs, there will be a movement, already suggested by Etzioni and Logan Wilson, to place Black urban youth into two-year community colleges. We mentioned the California tier system of admissions, which resulted in the following Black enrollments in the various higher educational institutions of that state: 6.1 per cent in community colleges, 2.9 per cent in the State colleges, and 0.8 per cent in the University of California. We know that more than half of Black youth entering colleges across the country are being placed into community colleges. It is also clear that community colleges, which usually have both a two-year liberal arts transfer curriculum and vocational tracks, have much higher attrition rates than four-year institutions. Yet, the Carnegie Commission on Higher Education has recommended that some 230 to 280 new community colleges be created within the next ten years, a large number of them in urban areas.[30] The Commission's line is echoed by Sidney P. Marland, present Commissioner of Education, who has placed a great emphasis on postsecondary vocational training as an alternative to universal four-year college training. This movement must be stopped dead in its tracks by the Black community, lest the two-year colleges become replicas of urban high schools. No amount of literature on the merits of community colleges can negate the fact that they exist primarily for students deemed intellectually unworthy of admission to four-year institutions. Access to urban community colleges for Black students is only motivated by the assessment by whites that these colleges are no longer useful for their children. Black students are being directed into two-year colleges precisely at that point in time when B.A.s and M.A.s are becoming the keys to an adequate livelihood in this society. Moreover, the present existence in two-year colleges of an almost totally white and *tenured* faculty body is simply not conducive to the flexible academic programming necessary to accommodate underprepared urban Black students.

What, then, is the answer? Either one can surrender to the Jensen–Stanley arguments and despair of ever breaking the vicious educational cycle, or one can accept the fact that high school records and S.A.T. scores are simply indices of the victimization of Black youth by their educational and social environments and therefore tell us nothing of the potential for academic growth of a particular Black student. If one accepts the latter view, then a change in the environment may well bring about a measurable change in the student's academic performance. Before me is the transcript of a 1964 Black and poor graduate of a Black New York high school. His high school average was 67. His graduating college average is "C." Among his grades are "As" in advanced elective courses in Shakespeare, the nineteenth-century novel, and two courses in poetry writing. His average in his English major is B+. Replicate this transcript a hundred times and one has a better sense of the talent buried under Sowell's and Etzioni's term "unqualified." At the City College of New York, the pioneer in the field of compensatory education, some 30 to 35 per cent of the "unqualified" students in its SEEK program are graduating from the college. This is to be matched against a national graduation rate of 50 per cent of all entering college freshmen.

The background of this and other compensatory education programs gives some clues as to the type of admissions procedure and structure that makes sense if the students are admitted to a predominantly white campus. First, the students should represent a broad spectrum of high school achievement, ranging from those who marginally meet the college's requirements for admission to those who in no case would previously have been considered for admission to the college. On the other hand, to enroll a homogeneous group of underprepared students with averages between 65 and 70 will almost certainly guarantee failure of the program, since peer pressure will tend to be absent.

After admission, it is imperative that time, work, and attention be dedicated to each student's specific needs by the college. If the most serious defect in the student's high school experience was the lack of a structured—and thus caring—environment, then the college must create a structure, preferably of departmental status, that devotes itself exclusively to developing the academic skills of the students. The first task of the department should be to analyze, through tests, the student's levels of achievement in reading, writing, and mathematics. A sequence of college preparatory courses should then be established in each of these areas so that students who need to upgrade their skills may do so before any contact with the regular college curriculum. The placement of students in courses and curricula must be flexible. Some, according to the test scores, may be placed in a limited number of regular courses, but with concentrated tutorial assistance. But in no case should a student with a ninth-grade reading level be placed in a course such as History I. He will invariably fail the course. Instead, colleges should devise special paced-down content courses that join the original course content with training in note-taking, essay examinations, and recognition of connections between lectures and assigned readings.

The college preparatory sequence should be intensive and of such dimensions as to keep the student well occupied with academic skill-building during most of the week. If the college's regular English composition course meets three times a week, the preparatory course should meet six times a week with class sizes half that of the regular courses. All of the preparatory work should carry some college credit: beyond the fact that any well-constructed preparatory course should contain college level materials, students will be more motivated if they are awarded credit. The key to successful compensatory education is never to look backward at the high school curriculum, but instead to look forward, determining what skills and abilities are necessary for successful work in college and building the compensatory curriculum around those needs. Attendance regulations for college preparatory courses ought to be strict, and students who ignore those regulations should be dropped from a course. Students must understand that although they cannot fail any of the college preparatory courses, they will receive no credit for a course and will be forced to repeat it unless sufficient progress is made. At the end of the first semester, a complete assessment in writing should be required from each instructor. On the basis of these evaluations, a student should either continue in the college preparatory curriculum, be moved into regular college work, or perhaps proceed with a program combining compensatory and regular college courses.

Colleges cannot expect miracles to be wrought overnight. It is important that students be given time to prove whether or not they are capable of obtaining a bachelor's degree. Therefore they should not be under the jurisdiction of regular college course and standing committees. The decision to drop students for academic reasons should rest in the hands of the department concerned with their college preparatory work only after two years of work, at the least. This department, however, has to take its responsibilities seriously. The academic progress of each student should be constantly monitored, and students who show no signs of forward movement after sufficient time should first be placed on probation, and then dropped. The environment permeating the college preparatory department should be at the same time both supportive and demanding. Every program should meet each student at his own level and lead him as far as possible academically without premature penalties or experiences of failure.

Students already disenchanted with the high school curricula need some motivational stimulus to initially arouse their interest in academic matters. The college preparatory curriculum should be laced through with materials to which the students can relate. The program must also emphasize and believe in the intrinsic worth of the students' own thoughts and writing, no matter how ungrammatically expressed. This cannot be a gratuitous and patronizing act of kindness, for the Black student brings with him both a creativity and a knowledge of the human condition unduplicable by white middle-class students. Some examples of essays written at the beginning and end of a compensatory English course by "underprepared" Black students suffice to make the point:[31]

Example 1

Beginning of Semester

Harlem taught me that light skin Black people was better look, the best to succeed, the best off fanicially etc this whole that I trying to say, that I was brainwashed and people aliked.

I couldn't understand why people (Black and white) couldn't get alone. So as time went along I began learned more about myself and the establishment.

End of Semester

In the midst of this decay there are children between the ages of five and ten playing with plenty of vitality. As they toss the football around, their bodies full of energy, their clothes look like rainbows. The colors mix together and one is given the impression of being in a psychadelic dream, beautiful, active, and alive with unity. They yell to each other increasing their morale. They have the sound of an organized alto section. At the sidelines are the girls who are shy, with the shyness that belongs to the very young. They are embarrased when their little dresses are raised by the wind or they are delighted when trying on high heels and lipstick. As their feet rise above the pavement, they cheer for their boy friends. In the midst of the decay, children will continue to play.

EXAMPLE 2

Beginning of Semester

The whole experiences was one of completeness; completeness in the senses that I experienced a different way of living on the Western Coast. The people were very neighorly which give me a feeling of welcome after evaluating the attitudes of the people around me; I discover that the main cause of their behavior were ones mainly because of the pace of life. Most are productive; but very few seem to be in a great hurry; seem in its' self sit a tone which seem peaceful.

End of Semester

Richards story "The Voodoo of Hell's Half Acre" was his first attempt to accomplish something without the aid of family or friends. The fact that he wrote a story was symbolic to his associates. Richard's friends had accepted their limitations assigned to them by society. But Richard wasn't conforming to the norms of society, thus causing ill feeling toward him. Richard had thought that perhaps by writing a story, he could make himself acceptable. However, this event caused his friends to cut Richard off completely.

EXAMPLE 3

Beginning of Semester

For my ninth grade of school my mother deceided to send my brother and I away to a borden school; in the south, mainly because my brother was doing so poorly in his subject. And I being a very quiet withdraw (hard to make friend) young girl; she thought an different atmosphere woold help us both.

I spent almost two years at Laurinburg Institute. I live with about 50 girl. They were from all parts of the United States. I encounted so many different personality that I had not choice but to accept and learned to like these girl.

End of Semester

My classroom is sort of small with dimensions of about twenty by eighteen feet. It has a low ceiling and only one entrance. Once the door is closed it seems as if you have been removed from the usual city classroom, giving an air of warmth and congeniality. The four corners overlap as though the architect intended to make it a square and changed his mind. The spring green color of the walls. though aged, along with the low ceiling and closeness gives the classroom a cottage type atmosphere.

Looking out the window increases the feeling of having been removed from the bustle of the city. As the actor is accepting a standing ovation from the balcony, the tall trees are standing full and strong with their thousands of leaves clapping and their greenness touching the blue sky. Yet they're not overpowering or really close because the sun shines brightly and the sunbeams glitter and glisten through the multiple squares of glass, on to the students and the clutter of wooden furnishing and the spring green walls as it holds the chalk dust in mid-air.

Thus, the task of any program is to maintain and strengthen the creativity of the Black student, while at the same time guiding him to a knowledge of those rules of grammar and rhetoric that will better permit him to express himself clearly and precisely.

It should also be clear that the staff of such a program should be chosen with great care. First, they must have a knowledge base and teaching experience. Second, they must have a determined belief in the potential of the students to succeed in college. Third, they must demand performance from the students. A crippling development in the growth of E.O.P. programs has been the recruitment of young graduate students, most frequently white radicals, so torn with guilt and unconscious racism that they have told their Black students that there is no necessity for them to learn the rules of grammar since those rules are a reflection of the "cultural imperialism" of white America. In this context, I can scarcely forget a conversation with the director of a compensatory math program, well on his way to a Ph.D. in physics, at a large state university. He declared that he did not encourage Black students to take mathematics, even if their achievement level was that of the seventh grade. The students, he said, disliked and feared mathematics and were more content with courses in the humanities and drama. He saw no need to impose his views about the value of mathematics onto students who were uncomfortable with the discipline.

The attitudes that such teachers bring to the class are perversions of the pioneering work of such persons as Beryl Bailey, Carol Reed, and William A. Stewart, originators of what is now popularly called the concept of "Black English" or "Black dialect." Their efforts were directed toward establishing the fact that the urban Black youth speaks a variety of English that is internally consistent in its grammatical and rhetorical structure. They move from that point to argue that the teachers of such students should respect the language in which the child was raised. They have also attempted to pinpoint those particular characteristics of the "dialect" that most interfere with the Black students' ability to learn standard English. By so doing, they hope to create new methods of teaching standard English to Black students. But none of the three would argue that an urban Black student should not constantly be moving toward a mastery of the English language. At Laney Junior College in California, one instructor was quoted as saying, "We shouldn't impose standard English, but we shouldn't deny it to those who want it." [32] The net result of this and similar approaches to the education of underprepared Black students is to leave them functionally illiterate.

College preparatory programs must have a large number of Black teaching faculty and should be headed by a Black administrator. This leads to the question of the national lack of Blacks with Ph.D. degrees, and to the consequent necessity for finding alternative criteria for college teaching appointments. There are, throughout the country, hundreds of Blacks without the Ph.D., but frequently possessing M.A.s, who are creative, academically productive, vital to the present Black movement, and capable of teaching not only college preparatory courses but also many of the courses in the traditional curriculum now taught by white Ph.D.s with little concern for teaching Blacks or whites. If such persons are hired to do a task to which the college is committed and gives priority, they should undoubtedly have the same titles, ranks, and promotional opportunities as other members of the faculty. If colleges have long waived academic credentials for professors in the performing arts, physical education, or the ROTC, why should it be so difficult to waive requirements for Blacks doing the most important educational work in the college? If the college, however, cannot escape from its fixation on the Ph.D. degree, then the institution should create procedures whereby Black faculty would receive paid sabbaticals to work toward the degree. Persons teaching college preparatory courses in such fields as mathematics and English should hold either an appointment in the regular academic department or a joint appointment in the academic department and the college preparatory department. In the former case, appointments should be mutually acceptable to both departments.

Nothing in the above should be construed to mean that Blackness should be the sole criterion for appointment or reappointment to teaching or administrative positions. If, in fact, the program is poorly administered or teachers prove incapable or unwilling to do the job of building up the academic skills of the students, then they should be removed, regardless of color, charisma, or ability to rap with students. The educational needs of Black youth are too pressing to be sacrificed to manifest incompetence.

Besides structure, relevant curricula, and a good teaching staff, a strong counseling system is needed, preferably at a 50:1 ratio that encourages a relationship between a single person and a student from the day of his arrival on campus. A counselor ought to be mature, experienced, and prepared to deal with any problem that hinders the academic progress of the student. Such problems will range from an inability to concentrate on lectures to serious medical problems. There is a large number of Black social workers with masters' degrees in social work who have dedicated their lives to helping the poor Black urban family break the cycle of poverty. This group may provide a valuable source of trained counselors. They know the environment from which the students come; and, unlike psychological counselors, they are trained to assist actively in the solution of a problem. For this very reason, the recruitment of young, untrained, college graduates as full-time counselors should be discouraged, although peer counseling may prove a useful complementary device for assisting the students to adjust to college life. There should always be some counselors trained in psychological therapy for those few students who may be in need of such assistance. The functions of the counselors must be well defined. They should bear complete responsibility for the student's academic programming, meet regularly with the student, consult with the teaching faculty about the student's progress, be alert for signs of absenteeism, and consult with the program's administration on all matters concerning the student's academic standing. In short, the counselor binds the student to the college.

Professor Etzioni states without sympathy that students in compensatory education programs require "even living allowances." [33] Of course they do! For if Black urban students had the financial resources available to white middle-class youth, then there would be no urban problem. The students need not only remission of tuition, payments for books, and fees, but also stipends that frequently go above the level necessary for their own sustenance because they have to contribute to the support of their families. "Living allowances" have long been given to millions of white students, but in their cases they were called "scholarships." [34]

If a college created a program of the type outlined in the past few pages and still failed to succeed in graduating substantial numbers of Black youth, then one might well question the premises of this author. But to his knowledge, few colleges have followed such a pattern. The one that has come the closest, the City College of New York, in its SEEK program, has come up with convincing evidence that the task of upgrading the academic skills of Black urban youth can be done.

6

Blackening the Curriculum

White Universities and Black Studies

Once an institution committed itself to the admission and academic support of underprepared Black students, a question immediately arose as to the curriculum the students would follow after they had completed the college preparatory program.

Most white administrators and professors seemed to operate on the premise that Black students would quietly enter into the traditional academic disciplines. Given the strong Black Power movement developing in the Afro-American community, which coincided with the arrival of the students on campus, this was impossible. Furthermore, even white students were expressing dissatisfaction with the traditional curriculum during the years 1967 to 1970.

The movement for Black studies cannot totally be related to contemporary issues, of course, since both Carter Woodson and Du Bois had long searched, unsuccessfully, for an educational curriculum and an institutional setting for the "special education" of Black youth. No Black institution in the South had been able to provide its own specialized curriculum as had, for example, the network of Catholic colleges across the country. The thrust for a "relevant" Black education came, therefore, from students on predominantly white campuses, since it was precisely there that the contradictions between white and Black America were most intense. The white American university has always been preoccupied with Western civilization and has refused, over decades, to deal seriously with the question of Black people in this country. How, one might ask, could Professors Glazer, Banfield, and Wilson, in view of their writing on urban affairs, help a Black student at Harvard who wanted to study the Black condition in cities?

White Americans, moreover, have grown up with teachers, parents, and commencement speakers pounding home the fact that "education is power." Philosophers from Plato to Dewey have emphasized education's function as a socializing mechanism for a nation's youth. It was not strange, then, that Black students felt a compelling force enveloping them when they entered into courses on the Renaissance, Locke, Hume, Thoreau, and Melville. Many of them sensed that this traditional liberal arts curriculum (with its attendant emphasis on rights, consensus, due process, etc.) was aimed at reconciling them to the status quo and giving them the intellectual sophistication with which to view objectively, i.e., neutrally, the social ills which plague America. Yet they were the daily victims of those "social ills," along with their families and friends.

While the traditional curriculum of the university might well give a white job-oriented striver a clear answer to his identity and role in society, it could give no such answer to a Black student and, by its content, almost defied him to raise the question in an intellectually respectable manner. Thus, at a crucial moment in a youth's development, the tradition-bound educational process lays down a well-defined and severely constricted path to success in the society which he often cannot even follow.

Many Black students, thrust into this mechanism, felt they had to make a choice between "success" and integrity, a fact which might well explain the intensity of their demands for Black studies programs. Black studies presented to the university a complex set of problems. First, there was serious doubt among academicians that any such body of knowledge as "Black studies" existed. Second, many scholars felt that the programs would be highly politicized and doctrinaire. Third, a fear existed that the

quality of the programs would be inferior since there was a severe shortage of scholars, Black or white, trained in the discipline. Fourth, there was a concern over dangers to academic
freedom implicit in the student demands for complete autonomy
of the program, both in faculty selection and in course offerings.
Fifth—and this objection came primarily from Black integrationists—there was an uneasy sense that Black studies was only
a device for diverting Black students away from the conquest of
the "hard" disciplines into a dead-end curriculum that would
ultimately be of no value either to them or to the Black community. Finally, questions arose over the proposed exclusion of
white students and white professors from Black studies programs.

A conference held at Yale University in the spring of 1968, on
the subject of Black studies, gave indications of the concern felt
by white academics about many of the issues raised above.[1] One
unidentified professor asked Harold Cruse, the noted Black historian and social analyst: "Are you asking that the university
accept these courses *despite* the fact that they contain an ideological bias . . . If that is what you mean, how do you justify
it? Do you insist that these courses must be taught by black
people? And why?" [2]

Another questioner, perplexed about the ideological thrust of
Black studies, stated that if the curriculum were to be "confused
with the notion of revolutionary commitment, then we may end
up with a sort of educational disaster." [3] Speaking to the same
point, McGeorge Bundy declared that "there is nothing wrong
with providing a sense of direction, identity, and purpose; but
it is a very dangerous thing to start pushing the subject around
for that purpose." [4] Reflecting on earlier remarks of Gerald A.
McWorter, Bundy continued: "The question does arise . . .
whether the subject is fit yet for effective teaching in our colleges and universities—not because it lacks size or meaning, but
because the instruments of teaching, the bibliographic and library tools, and above all the properly trained and qualified instructors do not exist." [5]

The most sweeping white attack on the Black studies concept
came from Eugene Genovese, a scholar of Black history, in an
article published in *The Atlantic Monthly* in June 1969.[6] With-

out hesitation, he plunged into the heart of debate around Black studies, declaring that the demands for autonomy and for an exclusively Black faculty were, in fact, demands that indicated that the programs would be ideologically oriented.[7] He further argued that there was no Black ideology and therefore "what the Blacks want is almost invariably what the dominant faction in a particular Black caucus wants."[8] Turning to the issue of faculty quality, Genovese declared that the hiring of faculty who would not ordinarily qualify for professorial status represented a "general contempt for all learning and a particular contempt for black studies as a field of study requiring disciplined, serious intellectual effort . . ." He ended his argument by condemning the proposed use of Black studies as a psychological prop for Black students.[9]

The Black integrationist opposition to the Black studies movement came primarily from Black academicians such as Kenneth Clark and W. Arthur Lewis, as well as Roy Wilkins of the NAACP.[10] Basic to all of their arguments was the assumption that voluntary segregation of Blacks in Black studies programs was supportive of white racism, in that it permitted the university to continue its general practices without facing the necessity for integration of all aspects of college life. W. Arthur Lewis and Roy Wilkins were particularly concerned that the movement of large numbers of Black youth into Black studies programs would handicap those students later, when they would be forced to compete with whites who had used college as a means of acquiring professional skills. Lewis emphasized the fact that the Black community was not self-sustaining and that, therefore, "Whether we like it or not, most Afro-Americans *have* [emphasis his] to work in the integrated world, and if we do not train for superior positions there, all that will happen is what happens now—that we shall be crowded into the worst paid jobs."[11] An almost unbridgeable ideological gap appeared to divide the integrationists from Black separatists, yet both had as a common goal the preparation of Blacks for leadership.

The imprimatur of academic respectability was placed upon Black studies with Harvard's announcement in January 1969 that it would move toward the creation of an Afro-American Studies Department. The Black studies programs that emerged across the country were of startlingly different patterns. At Federal City College in Washington, for example, there was a total four-year program, with all courses required, directed toward the "de-colonization" of the minds of Black students and a reorientation of them toward becoming "skilled technicians ideologically committed to the creation of a viable African nation." Students were to be plunged into a four-year sequence that emphasized the communality of the problems of African peoples, whether they be on the Continent, in the Caribbean, or in the United States. There was a major emphasis on the creation of skills that seemed to be of immediate value to the Black community. At Harvard, in contrast, the traditional program concentrated on Black history, literature, and politics, with some attention to field work in the Black community.[12] The Berkeley program differed from both Federal City College and Harvard in that its principal thrust was toward the Black community in urban areas, with less stress on history, and strong emphasis on Black literature and arts. Nationwide, there seemed to be a common core of subjects that included African History, Afro-American History, Black Literature, Psychology of Racism, History of Black Thought, Education in the Black Community, Afro-American Music, the Black Family, the Communications Media and the Black Community, and Economics of the Black Community, with additional work in seminars and a field-work component.

At this point, there can be and should not be any conclusions drawn as to the viability of Black studies as an academic discipline. From the outset there has been an unsteady and faltering growth of the programs resulting from a combination of factors: overt and covert white academic resistance to the programs; Black students' demands for instant departments; the absence of a sufficient number of Black scholars to staff dozens of departments; struggles within the programs among faculty and students as to the definition of Black studies; and excessive and erratic Black student control over Black faculty.

The white resistance to Black studies is most clearly evident in the areas of financing and structuring of many of the programs. Administrations, in the heat of 1968–69, promised the moon to Black students. Once the programs were in operation and the students' voices had softened, Black studies directors found that their programs frequently were, as one stated, "underfinanced and understaffed." [13] Moreover, the organizational structure of some programs, instead of being departmentalized, was such as to leave actual control over course offerings and faculty appointments in the hands of the traditional academic departments while naming some Black person as "coordinator" or "director" of the program. At Vanderbilt University, where such a situation existed, the Black studies director had suggested an eminent African historian, Stanlake Samkange, winner of the Melville Herskovits Award for African History for his book *The Origins of Rhodesia*, for a full-time appointment to the history department. The department refused to offer a full-time appointment, proffering instead a one-semester visiting professorship because "some of the history professors were concerned that Samkange is a bit too militant by Vanderbilt standards. Others, ignoring Samkange's awards, his impressive list of publications, and their own lack of expertise in his field, criticized his scholarship."[14]

In other instances, college presidents faced with the choice of Black studies directors made ludicrous selections. I can think of no more outstanding case of this sort than the selection at one university of a Black studies director with a B.A., and a background not remotely connected either to scholarship or the Black community over a famous Black literary critic and poet, possessor of a Ph.D., and the author of six books in his specialty.

It is impossible, in view of the paucity of written information on white reactions to Black studies programs, to document the full range of "treatments" given these programs. But conversations with Black studies directors from around the country indicate that a variety of roadblocks were erected against the development of the programs. These ranged from a refusal by the colleges to provide secretarial services, telephones, and office space to attempts by regular departments to duplicate, course by course, the offerings of Black studies departments in an effort to draw students away from the programs.

One cannot, however, blame white administrators for that natural instinct toward self-preservation which led to the overnight creation of Black studies programs. Black students deeply felt the immediate need for Black studies for their own survival, and likewise college presidents felt that it was in the interests of *their* survival to give the students what they wanted. The problems which arose because of this feeling of urgency remain, and they still leave their marks on the programs today. Few college administrators would introduce a new program, for example, in Latin American studies without a year's lead-time—or more. During that time, they would make an extensive search for the best man in the country to serve as the chairman of the department. They would then leave it to the chairman to recruit his faculty and develop the course structure of the program. There would be an assumption on the part of the administration that the chairman knew his field, and there would be no demand that the first-year offerings constitute the entire program. The chairman would be given two to three years to develop the total curriculum, depending on the availability of persons qualified to teach particular specialties within the area.

Such was not the case with Black studies. By the summer of 1969, literally hundreds of colleges were searching desperately for Blacks acceptable to the students, with any knowledge whatsoever of Afro-American or African affairs, who would be prepared to create a Black studies major within a year. Once hired, the professors found themselves called upon to develop a curriculum with the collaboration of students who may or may not have agreed among themselves as to what constitutes Black studies. In many cases, the results were a potpourri of offerings without a central theme.

Nowhere was the lack of Black ideological consensus more evident than in the matter of Black studies. It was as if a man were leaning against a door which suddenly opened and revealed five other opened doors all leading to different precious gems, but one could choose only one door. Some colleges chose to emphasize Pan-Africanism, others the Black experience in America, still others concentrated on contemporary Black life in urban areas, while some programs were deep into "Third Worldism." White administrators, moreover, had given Black students considerably more power over faculty in Black studies programs than students exerted over professors in the traditional disciplines. In many cases, the students' choice of faculty was exemplary, but in others, poor. The rapidity with which ideological shifts were taking place within the Black community meant that a Black studies director, originally hired by students oriented toward Pan-Africanism, could find himself ousted by new students who had become "Third World" oriented. The net result of the changing moods was to make the academic life of many a Black studies professor "short, nasty, and brutish" as he failed to make his course "relevant" to the students.

It is also clear that the growth of the programs was hampered by the absence of a sufficient number of Black scholars to staff the departments. There were plenty of Black people in this country capable of repeating endlessly the phrases of Malcolm X and Frantz Fanon, but there was a distinct lack of Black persons trained in the critical areas of Afro-American and African history, which should be the very core of a Black studies program. A Ford Foundation survey of 1968 indicated that over the five years from 1964 to 1968 some 350 Ph.D.s were awarded to Blacks, 0.78 per cent of all Ph.D.s granted during this time.[15] Even if one adds to the potential pool of Black studies faculty such distinguished Black historians as John Henrik Clarke, who does not hold an earned Ph.D. degree but has received an honorary doctorate, the number of Black scholars is insufficient to satisfy the demands of Black students throughout the country for Black studies programs.

Du Bois and Woodson originally posed the question of a "special" education to be given to Black students. Shifted into a contemporary context, the problem is, how should Black students be educated within a white academic framework. But to answer this question is to ask another: "Education for what?" Some might have an easy and quick retort to the query: "Black liberation." But if one probes into the meaning of "Black liberation," its definition can be as diverse as: economic, social, and political equality for Black people in America within an integrated context; a separate Black nation in the South; unification of the African continent; or the creation of an interlocking network of Black-controlled cities within the United States. Now, no one can predict the future of Black people in America, but I am haunted by the realities of the condition of Black life in urban areas and the almost total dependency on the white economy for a meager daily sustenance. And my immediate answer to the question of Black liberation would be the elimination of their impoverishment. If one accepts this assumption—and it does not obviate any of the alternatives outlined above—then an educational strategy can begin to be developed. The core of this strategy would be the preservation by Black people of the broadest number of educational options possible for our students. And within these options, there should be an almost fanatical demand for the best possible academic training.

What implications would such a strategy have for Black studies programs? The first would be the recognition that out of mistakes one can build strength. It was probably inevitable that Black studies programs would evolve in the somewhat chaotic manner that they have. But lessons have been learned. The first is that some Black students on small, isolated, white campuses will just have to reconcile themselves—for the present—to the absence of a Black studies program. They may choose instead to create their own study seminars, have visiting lecturers, or spend an exchange year at a major campus that does have a Black studies program. At large white institutions, and particularly in public metropolitan colleges, Black studies should be available for students. In some cases, this may necessitate a pooling of the academic resources of neighboring urban institutions so as to create viable programs. To ensure the quality of both staff and programs of Black studies, a national accrediting agency, along the lines of the Institute of the Black World in Atlanta, might be given the task of accrediting the programs, thus signaling to both students and graduate schools that the degree being offered is academically valuable.

There are also ways of hastening the production of scholars of Blackness. For example, at present many Black studies professors hold degrees in such disciplines as sociology, political science, or English, and have come only lately to the study of Black people. College- or foundation-funded programs which would permit them to enroll at the Institute of the Black World for a year of retooling and study would be valuable. Along the same lines, monies should be made available to create seven or eight major metropolitan centers of Black studies with undergraduate, graduate, and research components. This project ought to proceed slowly but well, so that within the next five years we will be able to see a steady flow of Black scholars to colleges around the country.

If Black studies is to be a viable discipline, then there must be a recognition that until *someone* comes up with an all-embracing ideology, there must be room in the same department for community development specialists and Pan-Africanists, Ph.D.s in history and economics, and master teachers of Black children in the elementary schools. All the professors should be highly competent and "qualified" in their fields, learned as well as sympathetic. Speaking of his pioneering study on the *Philadelphia Negro* in his autobiography, W. E. B. Du Bois stated: "First of all, I became painfully aware that merely being born in a group, does not necessarily make one possessed of complete knowledge concerning them." [16]

The real end of Black studies is not therapy but education to give young Black people a solidly grounded knowledge in things Black as well as a conceptual framework within whose contours they can begin to develop their own strategies for solving the problems of the Black urban masses. In this context it is absolutely necessary that courses be rigorously constructed and that they provide the broadest possible exposure to all schools of Black thought. Certainly, practically every professor of the social sciences or humanities in this country approaches his courses with a bias. It shows in his choice of books, the topics he chooses to emphasize in his lectures, and the manner in which he interprets the major sources in his field. In European universities, one frequently encounters the phenomenon of professors, avowedly Communists, who teach courses in history from an entirely Marxist perspective. In America, one need only look at the curriculum of some Catholic universities, or of Yeshiva, to recognize the obvious indoctrinating intent of their courses of study. In fact, no professional academician approaches any subject without an interpretive overview that he conveys to his students. Basic and necessary to good teaching, however, is the obligation of a professor to expose a student first to all the facts pertinent to the subject under scrutiny and second to the various schools of criticism as they interpret those facts. Having done this, the professor should be free to examine critically and freely both the facts and the scholarly interpretations of those facts. And the students, likewise, should be encouraged to argue and question the assumptions and ideology of professors and books as they deal with the topic under discussion. These techniques must be followed in the case of Black studies. Within the context of Black togetherness, the broadest possible discussion and intellectual stimulation must take place lest the students be stifled. They must be given the opportunity to find new ways of interpreting the Black experience which may lead to different solutions from those presently proposed by the Black intelligentsia.

The primary goal of Black studies programs, of course, is to produce Black studies majors who might either go on to graduate school or begin working in the Black community. But there are an infinite number of programs sponsored by the department beyond that goal. First, white colleges might be persuaded to allow Black students to take African or Afro-American history as a substitute for the traditional requirement of Western civilization or American history. Students wishing to be teachers could major in Black studies with a minor in education. Likewise, Black pre-med students could take field-work courses in the health needs of the Black community as an adjunct to their major in chemistry or biology. Black studies departments must always be open to the possibilities of a major in Black studies with a minor in economics, political science, or psychology; I, for one—years before the Black studies movement arose—was extremely leery of any student graduating from college without a firm background in some discipline. Indeed, one could argue that Black students' programs that look only inward will be, in the long run, deleterious to the interests of Black people. There should be a course on "economics" of the ghetto, but it should move outward from the ghetto to indicate the economic factors that regulate life in the inner cities. No Black student should emerge from college without knowing the sources and manifestations of white power that daily impinge upon the Black community. To call that power irrelevant to one's education is self-destructive. The critical tension that produced the earlier Black historical renaissance was founded precisely on the confrontation of young Blacks with white scholarship. Ignorance of the Industrial Revolution or of the development of both capitalist and socialist theory is simply not conducive to creating a cadre of young people capable of building a nation.

In all probability, the majority of Black students will continue to major in traditional disciplines while taking some courses in Black studies. Most likely both the short- and the long-range goals of the Black community will be best served by such a choice. There is appalling disparity between the number of Blacks and whites in such fields as physics, economics, mathematics, biology, and chemistry—the areas where exciting and potentially dangerous research activities are taking place. When one considers the awesome discoveries of recent years in genetics concerning the possibility of gene manipulation, then it becomes imperative that Blacks be cognizant of the implications of such discoveries for Black people. In the same fashion, the Black community needs doctors, architects, and engineers. In brief, the primary thrust of Black education in white institutions should be toward the conquest of those academic disciplines that will best permit the students to deal with the white world. That path leads directly to a confrontation by Black students with disciplines from which few have traditionally graduated.

It would be sanguine to assume that all the students who today talk of returning to the community will do so. Many will, of necessity, take employment with white firms. But I have no particular worry over the growing numbers of Black professionals employed in the white sector of the economy. It is almost certain that experiences in such environments will heighten their Black consciousness and force them to realize that their fate is inextricably tied to that of the Black urban poor. The innate racism of white society will take care of that problem.

To this day there have been no Black institutions of higher education. It is conceivable that a college could be created which would provide both the technical skills and the ideological framework of an entirely different education, superior to that offered in white institutions. One has in mind the fledgling development of such a university as Malcolm X Liberation University in North Carolina, which has as its end "the training of technicians who will work to deal with the basic needs of our people, not that of technocrats who will act as 'slave masters by proxy' and neo-colonist administrators." [17] Building on the concept of the African extended family unit, the university, for example, would attempt to train a doctor *only to make a living and not accumulate great wealth, and in turn for his service, the Black Community would support him.*" The curriculum is highly disciplined and combines training in some skill—food scientists, architects, teachers—within a context of Pan-Africanism. It is uncertain whether the university will fail or succeed in its mission, but the very attempt to provide a structured and well-conceived alternative to traditional education is worthy of great praise and suggestive of similar efforts that could be mounted in large urban areas.

One could conceive of the construction over the next five years of a number of small urban experimental colleges that would be staffed exclusively by Blacks and serve only the Black community surrounding them. Such colleges should be small, at first, to escape the administrative chaos that surrounded the opening of Federal City College, which was to have been the prototype of this sort of institution. It should be emphasized also that Federal City College had a white president and a 50 per cent white faculty. The colleges envisaged here would have as their primary mission the education of the youth of the community, but would have tentacles reaching into every aspect of the life of the community. Its library would be open to the public and contain a children's reading room. Adjacent high schools and elementary schools would come under the jurisdiction of the college's school of education, and their students would spend at least half of their time teaching in the schools, working directly with pupils. Day-care facilities would be an integral part of the college, both for its students and for the community. A fully staffed health clinic would be housed in the college. At night and on Saturdays and Sundays, the college would be open for adults from the community who wished to earn a college degree or receive advanced training in their field of specialization. If adults in the community felt it impossible to reach the college, then the college would send professors to storefronts, where they would give instruction in the evenings. The college's auditorium would be freely available to any community groups needing it for a meeting place. If the community's impact on white or Black politicians was not strong enough, then professors from the college would lecture and teach various community groups the theory and practice of political strategies.

The college, ideally, would provide a full range of traditional disciplines, but with emphasis in every case on the implications for Black people. Thus, the traditional political science course would examine white authors, but always relate their writings to the condition of Black people throughout the world. First-year economics would give the students a thorough mastery of traditional economic theory, including all of Keynes, the multiplier effect and the accelerator, but would devote a major part of the course to the relationship between such theories and the economic dependency of African nations and Black Americans. Students would be required, as part of any program, to devote one day a week to unpaid work in the Black community—in schools, community centers, narcotics halfway houses, and so on. In time, professional schools of law, medicine, and business would be added to the university.

The faculty would be all Black and highly qualified in their specialties. Most would possess Ph.D. degrees—which, of course, would not be the sole criterion of appointment. They would have to be committed to building independent Black institutions, and to giving the best education possible to the youth entering the college, no matter how underprepared they seemed for college work. The present wave of Black students passing through college and graduate schools would provide both the ideological commitment and the basic knowledge necessary to create such a faculty body.

The reader may well ask in what way these institutions would differ from the segregated Black colleges in the South, both in regard to academic quality and to the possibility of unequal funding from state governments. As to the first point, we have already explicitly indicated that every attempt would be made to ensure that the academic quality of the institution would be outstanding. Moreover, as noted earlier, the Black colleges of the South performed an important educational service, given the fact that no white institution was willing to undertake the task of educating Black people. The same situation exists today with both Northern and Southern white colleges, unwilling to commit themselves totally to the higher education of the Black youth emerging from the deteriorating inner-city high schools. Even if they were willing to do so, it is still unlikely that they would be capable of doing the job successfully. We refer here not to the Black high school graduates with averages above 78, but to the masses of youth with averages between 65 and 75. One can only admit that the possibility exists that a Black urban college will be underfunded in relation to white institutions, but it is not sufficient reason to deter Black people from attempting to create alternative institutions that will seek new solutions to the higher educational needs of Black urban youth.

7

"It Can Mean, God Help Us, the Admission of Everybody!" Open Admissions

A Case Study in the Politics of Race in Higher Education

Perhaps no better example of the politics of race in higher education can be found than the open admissions policy of the City University of New York. We have constantly emphasized several factors involved in racial clashes on the campuses: the educational lag, measured in high school averages and S.A.T. scores between white and Black seniors; the relatively inflexible stance of white universities on admission standards; the instability of the campus environments into which newly recruited Black students entered; and the need for special structural devices for ensuring the success of underprepared Black students and the consequent uneasiness aroused among white faculty and administrators when such measures were taken. An examination of the genesis and development of the open admissions policy (O.A.P.) should lead the reader to a deeper appreciation of these problems. In this particular case study, New York's Puerto Rican community was involved together with the Black community in the struggle for access to higher education.

In 1968, the City University of New York, the world's largest municipal institution, consisted of nine senior colleges with a total enrollment of 46,800 undergraduates, six community colleges enrolling 15,000 students, and a graduate school with 1,000 doctoral candidates. The units were governed by a common board of trustees, the Board of Higher Education, whose members were appointed by the mayor of the city.

The system was diffuse, with each college having considerable autonomy governing its internal administrative and curricular affairs. The faculty was, in substantial proportions, inbred, since a large number of them were graduates of the municipal colleges with Ph.D. degrees obtained at either Columbia or New York University. There was, thus, a considerable degree of parochialism inherent in the attitudes of the faculties toward curricular matters.

If one had surveyed the course requirements in each of these institutions in the year 1968, he would have found a striking similarity among them, since they all derived from the curriculum requirements of City College, which had remained practically unchanged over thirty years. Within the system there was a schism between the senior colleges, which admitted students usually with averages above 82, and the community colleges, which admitted students below that average either to liberal arts programs that led to a transfer to the senior colleges after two years or to a terminal career or technical two-year degrees. Each of the senior colleges had erected substantial barriers to students wishing to transfer from the community colleges' liberal arts programs. These usually took the form of forcing community college transfer students to make up large numbers of courses that were required for graduation from the senior colleges but not required in the community college liberal arts programs. There was present, then, a snobbism among the senior college faculty about the question of standards even when 90 per cent of the community college students transferring to the senior colleges were white.

The university's faculty and student body, until 1964, was almost totally white. Of a faculty of three thousand in the senior colleges, only some thirty Blacks held full-time tenured positions in academic departments. The Black matriculated undergraduate population was less than 2 per cent of the combined student bodies. In 1964, however, under the impetus of editorials by the New York *Amsterdam News* [1] ("Now this bunch of intellectuals acts as if it believes that God himself should not be allowed to sit in a classroom at CCNY or Hunter unless he presents an affidavit showing he is white and able to meet the I.Q. tests laid down on this earth by the Board of Higher Education"), and pressure from Black state legislators, the board initiated the College Discovery Program, under which a small number of Black students (250) were to be admitted to the community colleges even though their high school averages would not ordinarily have gained them acceptance to those colleges. In 1965, the City College of New York began its SEEK program with 105 Black and Puerto Rican students, chosen because they showed academic potential despite poor over-all high school averages. By 1966, SEEK had become a university-wide operation, and within two years some 1,500 students were enrolled in senior colleges through the program. The university, therefore, was beginning to move in a direction that was responsive to the urban problem.

The "flagship," as some alumni call it, of the university was City College, founded in 1847 as the Free Academy. Over the years it had become known as the "proletarian Harvard," not so much because of the excellence of its faculty, but because the existence in the 1930s of a depression and restrictive quotas against Jews in many of the nation's colleges. Thus, City College received an influx of poor but brilliant students, predominantly Jewish, who went on to achieve great fame in later years. Among its alumni were Jonas Salk, Felix Frankfurter, Alfred Kazin, Daniel Bell, Richard Hofstadter, a Nobel Prize winner, and a host of other luminaries in the arts, sciences, and humanities. City College was the nation's leading producer of graduates who went on to obtain Ph.D. degrees. The alumni of the institution had great pride in the academic achievements of the institution and an almost fanatic attachment to an admissions system that promised every graduate of a city high school with an average over 82 entrance to a college, where he could receive a quality education without the payment of tuition fees. The system, in their eyes, was objective and made no distinctions among students on the basis of race or religion. Many of the faculty of City College in 1968 agreed with this position.

City College, however, unlike the other institutions in the university, was physically located in what became a Black and Puerto Rican community. It now stands on a hill overlooking central Harlem, but separated from it by a park. Unbeknownst to the predominantly white faculty of the college, Black authors such as John Killens, James Baldwin, and John Williams had frequently referred in their writings to the white citadel on the hill that was inaccessible to the Black population in whose midst it stood and whose taxes paid both for the education of the white students and the salaries of the white faculty and administrators.

The primary reason for the absence of Black students on the City College campus, before the introduction of SEEK, was the educational genocide occurring throughout the elementary and secondary schools of New York City. The college had traditionally required an academic high school diploma with an average of at least 82 for admission. Yet when one looked at the predominantly Black high schools in 1968, Benjamin Franklin had only 11 graduates out of 318 who met these criteria and Boys High in Brooklyn had only 7 graduates out of a total of 353 who could meet City College's admission standards. Furthermore, the attrition of Black students from the time of entry into high school to graduation was 50 per cent, as compared to a 13 per cent attrition for white students.[2] A study made in 1971 concluded that only 16 per cent of all the Black graduates of New York City high schools received averages of 80 or above, as compared with 50 per cent of all white graduates of the system.[3] Thus, there was an irreconcilable gap between the admission standards of CCNY and the Harlem community's sense that its children were being denied an equal opportunity for higher education.

City College had made a more determined effort than any other unit in the university to bridge this gap. By 1968, the SEEK program consisted of 600 students out of a total full-time student body of 10,000. The college's master plan called for a total SEEK program size of 1,200 students by 1975, a growth rate that would have resulted, over eight years, in a student body 10 per cent Black and 5 per cent Puerto Rican. While such an increase might have been appropriate for some colleges, it was inappropriate for an institution so near to Harlem.

Generally, during the years 1965 to 1968, as was the case on campuses throughout the country, Black and Puerto Rican students were, for the most part, uninvolved in the antiwar and student and faculty power movements that began to erupt on the City College campus. Student and faculty demonstrations against Dow Chemical and the ROTC led to an unstable atmosphere on the campus. A group of radical faculty members began pushing both for increased faculty rights vis-à-vis the administration and for strong administrative stands against the release of student class standings to draft boards and against the calling of the police onto the campus. Faculty who, two years later, would be bitterly opposed to open admissions, engaged in endless tirades against the administration, the power structure, and any other suitable object for their newly found sense of social conscience. Their social conscience did not extend to Black matters. Shortly after the assassination of Martin Luther King, Jr., in April 1968, I called together a group of the most "radical" white faculty members and asked them to support a proposal that would have mandated that the freshman class of September 1968 have a 25 per cent composition of Black and Puerto Rican students to be drawn from Harlem and East Harlem. Only one of the ten radical leaders in the room agreed to the proposal. One of those who opposed the plan stated that he would leave the university since these students would most certainly destroy the traditional academic standards of CCNY.

Little did this professor understand the ferocity of the storm that was approaching the campus. For the Black and Puerto Rican students on the campus, although small in proportion to the total student body, were extremely well organized, well led, and supported by a group of Black and Puerto Rican faculty who had been recruited to teach and counsel in the SEEK program. Moreover, the students, having experienced the effectiveness of the SEEK program in aiding them to overcome their own academic deficiencies, felt a moral obligation to increase the accessibility of college to their brethren who differed not one whit from them in academic, social, and economic background, but had failed, by reason of the lottery system of admission, to become SEEK students. Ironically, however, the first movement toward the eventual explosion on the campus came from the Du Bois Society, a white radical group on campus. In the fall of 1968, they presented the president with a list of demands for increased minority admissions and a School of Black and Puerto Rican Studies. A lull occurred until February of 1969, when a group of Black and Puerto Rican students occupied the office of the president for four hours, while presenting five demands:

1. That a School of Black and Puerto Rican Studies be established.

2. That a separate orientation program for Black and Puerto Rican students be established.

3. That students be given a voice in the administration of the SEEK program.

4. That the number of minority freshmen in the entering class reflect the 40–45 ratio of Blacks and Puerto Ricans in the total school system.

5. That Black and Puerto Rican history courses be compulsory for education majors and that Spanish language courses be compulsory for education majors.

The college remained quiet until the latter part of April when some 150 to 300 Black and Puerto Rican students occupied the South Campus, vowing to remain until such time as the demands were granted. The students remained on the campus in negotiation with the president for three weeks, until they were forced by court order to vacate the premises. Shortly thereafter, racial strife broke out between the Black and white students when some white male students physically attacked a group of Black female students. The police were then called to occupy the campus, the President resigned and was replaced by a biologist and conservative, who, during the latter part of May, succeeded in reviving negotiations between the Black and Puerto Rican community and faculty representatives on the issue of the demands. An agreement among these parties was reached on the two major issues: there was to be a School of Urban and Third World Studies, and an admission policy was devised that would have resulted by the fall semester of 1970 in a dual admissions system. Under the agreement, half of City College's freshmen were to have been admitted on the basis of grades and the other half on the basis of graduating from schools that traditionally had sent few of their graduates to college. In short, the students had won their demands.

Immediately upon announcement of the agreement—which still had to be ratified by the faculty senate and the Board of Higher Education—all of the mayoral candidates in New York City denounced the formula as a quota system. They were joined in the opposition by such City College alumni as Alfred Kazin, who stated, "I am thoroughly unhappy about any entrance to City College based purely on racial consideration." [4] The incoming president of the City College Alumni Association declared, "We are violently opposed to the breaking down of the standards of the school. We feel that open admissions would destroy the school rather than build it up."

The faculty of the college was divided over the merits of the proposal. One stated: "The proposal does necessitate a decrease in the number of merited admissions and a variety of racism, which must be abhorrent to any rational human being. It will result in a sharp decline in the standards of the college, or in setting up two colleges, neither of which will function effectively." [5]

Another said: "The admissions policy of the Black and Puerto Rican student community aims to correct the failure of opportunity. It does not impose any quota system. It seeks, rather, to offer a place in the college to public high school graduates whose potential has been masked by hopelessness and frustration." [6]

In early June, the faculty senate of CCNY rejected outright the negotiated agreement, using instead the time-honored device of appointing a committee to examine the "feasibility" of establishing a Black and Puerto Rican studies program, and substituting a pallid admissions formula that would have brought in 400 Black and Puerto Rican students in addition to those already admitted under the SEEK program.

The Board of Higher Education and the chancellor's office had been deeply involved in the issues raised by the students from the beginning of the occupation. It is no exaggeration to state that the atmosphere at the board in that spring of 1969 was akin in mood to that which must have prevailed in General Westmoreland's headquarters as the reports of the impact of the Tet offensive came in. For not only was City College in a state of siege, but almost every other institution in the university was being paralyzed by racial conflict, related both to admissions policies and to proposed Black studies programs. Although the City College faculty had temporized on the issue of admissions and Black and Puerto Rican studies, the chancellor and the board realized that there would be no peace in the university until some positive answers to the students' demands were forthcoming, and by July 1969, decisions had been reached on university policy toward the demands.

First, on the question of Black and Puerto Rican studies, the board committed itself to the creation of departments, institutes, or interdisciplinary programs in these areas within all of the senior colleges, but it specifically forbade the establishment of any "School of Ethnic Studies" until such time as the programs had proved themselves to be viable academically. On the most crucial matter, that of admissions policy, the board directed an earlier constituted Commission on Admissions to submit a report by October, in conformity with the following guidelines:

1. It shall offer admission to some university program to all high school graduates of the city.

2. It shall provide for remedial and other supportive services for all students requiring them.

3. It shall maintain and enhance the standards of academic excellence of the colleges of the university.

4. It shall result in the ethnic integration of the colleges.

5. It shall provide for mobility for students between various programs and units of the university.

6. It shall assure that all students who would have been ad-

mitted to specific community or senior colleges under the admissions criteria which we have used in the past shall be admitted. In increasing educational opportunity for all, attention shall also be paid to retaining the opportunities for students now eligible under present board policies and practices.

The board, in line with the political principle of not capitulating to pressure, said that it was simply advancing its already stated goal of open admissions by 1975 to the year 1970. Yet, the "open admissions" policy that had been laid out for 1975 was very different from that desired by the Black and Puerto Rican communities of New York City. For in the 1968 master plan of the university, a three-tiered California-type system had been established as the basis for the 1975 "open admissions program." Essentially, the top quarter of the city's high school graduates would have been admitted to the senior colleges; the middle portions of the graduating classes would have been admitted to community colleges; and the bottom quarter of the high school seniors would have been sent to "educational skills centers" that would have prepared them for vocational careers.

There was an admission on the part of the board that the Black and Puerto Rican students at City College had been the prime impetus for the change in the approach to the matter of enrollment policy. But, at the same time, by moving from a quota arrangement specifically designed to serve the needs of Black and Puerto Rican students to a position of open admissions, the board both diverted the thrust of the Black and Puerto Rican demands and gained a white middle-class constituency for the program. The contradictions implicit in the board's guidelines for open admissions meant that the Commission on Admissions became the primary arena in which the ethnic implications of the open admissions policy would be fought out. The guidelines also meant that the commission was deprived of the opportunity to deal honestly and broadly with the educational needs of the city's Black and Puerto Rican population. For there was an immense contradiction between the guideline calling for the ethnic integration of the colleges and that calling for an assurance that all students who would previously have been admitted to specific senior or community colleges would still be so admitted.

The dilemma into which the commission was thrust by the board's guidelines is highlighted by the following statistics, some prepared by the commission's staff and others garnered from subsequent studies. The public academic high schools of New York City were divided into three groups on the basis of the proportion of the graduating seniors from these schools who earned averages over 80 per cent or averages under 70. In Group I schools, 47 per cent of the seniors had averages over 80 per cent, while only 21 per cent had averages below 70. The comparable figures for Group II and III public high schools for graduating seniors with averages over 80 were 28 per cent and 13 per cent, and for seniors under 70, 34 per cent and 42 per cent. The ethnic composition of the three groups of schools, in descending order, was respectively 9 per cent, 23 per cent, and 58 per cent Black and Puerto Rican. The total of Black and Puerto Rican seniors in the system was 12,700, of whom only 1,600 were in Group I, and 4,500 in Group III schools. The majority of these students, some 6,600, were concentrated in Group II schools which, as previously indicated, were 76 per cent white. Within these schools, as in the other two categories of institutions, Blacks and Puerto Ricans were most likely to be found with low academic records.

This applied only to the *public* high schools. When one added to the pool eligible for open admissions the 21,000 graduates of nonpublic schools, which were well over 90 per cent white and comparable in the academic standing of their graduates to Group II schools, it is apparent that the commission had an impossible task on its hands were it to, at one and the same time, enhance ethnic integration and guarantee admission to a senior college to anyone who previously might have been eligible, i.e., any student with a high school average over 80. The hard fact—a replica of the national picture—was that one could not begin admitting large numbers of Black and Puerto Rican students into the senior colleges unless one dipped well below the 75 average, particularly since many of the Black and Puerto Rican graduates with averages over 80 were being recruited for colleges outside of New York City.

The commission, appointed by the board to design an allocation system for open admissions, consisted of thirty-eight persons, representing a diversity of forces in the university, including faculty, public officials, alumni, and representatives of the Black and Puerto Rican community, and ranging in political views from reactionary to white radical to Black militants. During the summer and early fall of 1969, the commission engaged in long and frequently acrid debates as to the criteria to be established for open admissions. The Blacks and Puerto Ricans, joined by some white radicals, argued for a total abolition of tests and high school averages as the basis for admission to the senior colleges. Instead, they would have substituted either a dual admissions system, such as that earlier proposed by the City College Black and Puerto Rican Coalition, or a totally random system of admission. The conservative white members of the commission, on their side, insisted on the sanctity of standards and bemoaned the fate of those white students from such famous academic high schools as the Bronx High School of Science who would be denied admission to the senior colleges under the plans espoused by the left wing of the commission.

Implicit in the approach to the problem of the left wing was an overriding commitment that the open admissions policy not result in a ghetto-ization of the community colleges and that each unit of the university have a heterogeneous mix of students. In the end, the commission was unable to agree on any one formula for admissions and instead submitted three plans to the board for consideration. Each of the plans envisaged an admission system based on a mixture of two criteria: a student's high school average and a student's rank in his graduating class. The SEEK admission procedure was to be used as a balancing device to bring about integration on the senior college campuses, since, as previously indicated, the majority of Black and Puerto Rican students were in integrated schools where they stood in the bottom halves of their classes.

The recommendations of the commission, transmitted to the Board of Higher Education in October 1969, aroused a public controversy of intense proportions. The *New York Times,* in an editorial, commented that the report was an "ideological jumble of good intentions . . . with considerations here obviously not academic, but rather how to achieve in each unit not merely integration, but a prescribed racial mix." [7] The proposals, concluded the *Times*, were "unfair to the best students because it would severely diminish their present options to enter those units of the City University with the highest academic standards." The faculty senate of the university, in a statement of policy, dismissed all three proposals and substituted its own recommendation which would have maintained the status quo.

The Board of Higher Education, in order to give the widest possible airing of the report's recommendation, held public hearings on the matter. In those hearings, two themes were constant from the white power structure of New York City: (1) There could be no "quota" system; (2) There could be no diminution of standards. On the Black and Puerto Rican side, there was an equally determined insistence that their children should have access to the senior colleges of the university and not be channeled into the community colleges. In a blunt statement, John Lindsay, then twelve days away from his election battle with a conservative Democrat, declared that: "In plain everyday language that means no quota system, that means no lottery system, that means every student who can now get into a senior college must be guaranteed a seat in a senior college. And, therefore, class rank cannot be used to govern admission to senior colleges." [8] The mayor's views were echoed repeatedly throughout the hearings.

The executive vice-chairman of the New York Board of Anti-Defamation League of B'nai B'rith said: "Ethnic balance is a euphemism for a quota system, a pernicious practice which we have traditionally and successfully opposed as being contrary to the democratic practice." [9] A professor representing the Brooklyn College "Faculty for Academic Excellence" observed: "It can mean, God help us, the admission of everybody." [10] A CCNY professor, referring to the SEEK program, said: "Well, it means that these loafers and so forth and incompetents had to be carried on. This is the atmosphere of students not quite prepared." [11]

These gentlemen and ladies were joined in their opposition to quotas by the president of the United Parents Association, a powerful educational lobby in New York City, by the principal of the elite Bronx High School of Science, and by innumerable representatives of Jewish community organizations.

The then-State Senator Basil A. Paterson was the major Black political spokesman for the commission's proposals:

I should tell you that the City College has much to do to make up for its previous one-hundred-year record as an almost one hundred per cent white institution in the midst of an almost one hundred per cent Black and Puerto Rican community. . . . I should like to make it clear that I will not be able to support any system of open admissions which turns out to be a continuation of the second-class, vocationally oriented, dead-end policy prevalent in our public high school system for Black and Puerto Rican youth. . . . We don't need an open admissions policy that is, in fact, a return to Booker T. Washington's philosophy. And if that be your intention, then you should forget the open admissions policy now and instead give us a Black University in Harlem and Bedford-Stuyvesant where we can turn our own energies to the education of these youth.[12]

So did the ethnic divisions in the City of New York manifest themselves once again. The controversy over the admissions report resolved itself into the simple question that pervades racial conflict over union membership, housing, executive employment, or teaching positions: are whites willing to give up something they monopolize in order to compensate Blacks for their long oppression by America?

The Board of Higher Education resolved the dilemma in November 1969 by rejecting the commission's proposals and substituting its own plan that did, however, incorporate the class ranking system proposed by the commission. The board's plan provided that all students applying to the university would be placed in one of ten parallel admissions groupings based either on high school average or ranking in one's own high school class. Thus, students who ranked either in the top tenth of their class or had a 90 per cent or higher average were placed in the top decile. Students in the fifth decile of their class were to be equated with students having a high school average of 80 or above. All such students were to be guaranteed admission to a senior college of the university. Students below these academic levels were to be placed into community colleges in the program of their choice, be it a liberal arts transfer program or a technical and terminal two-year program. The board's proposal placed great emphasis on student choice, which resulted in precisely the type of situation against which the left wing of the commission had warned. Under this policy, a student was given preference for admission to a particular senior or community college on the basis of his high school average or decile ranking. A phenomenon developed whereby certain senior colleges became the first choice of white students with high scholastic records, whereas other colleges received freshman classes that almost totally comprised students in the low 80 per cent category. Indeed, even with a sizable expansion in the SEEK program, some senior colleges had proportionately and absolutely fewer Black and Puerto Rican students under the open admissions than previously obtained. The prime beneficiaries, ironically, of the City College Black and Puerto Rican uprising were lower-middle-class whites. Moreover, several of the community colleges moved precipitously toward the 50 per cent point in the number of Black and Puerto Rican students in the total student body. In the face of these changes, the Board of Higher Education, in January 1972, moved to change the admissions policy in such a fashion as to make a more balanced distribution of students.

The board had barely had time to announce its decisions before a gaggle of major academic figures began to prophesy the demise of what had once been a great university. Notables such as Jacques Barzun, Robert Nisbet, and Irving Kristol held forth at length on this topic at a conference held in Washington, D.C., on October 29, 1971.[13] Like most educators across the country, these men were suffering under the delusion that the primary beneficiaries of open admissions were Black and Puerto Rican students, when, in fact, the vast majority of newly eligible students were white. Irving Kristol declared that there was an immutable correlation between socioeconomic class, performance on tests, and academic achievement. Said he, "We know that no educational program—anywhere, at any time, in this country or elsewhere—has ever been able to have a significant and enduring and extensive impact on these correlations."[14]

The main victims of the open admissions system, according

to Kristol, would be "qualified" Black and Puerto Rican students, since everyone would know that the university's degrees would not be worth the paper they were written on because the university would permit presumably "unqualified" [15] Black students to remain on campus for four years and give away diplomas gratis. Open admissions was for Kristol simply a sign "that the demands of some of our Black students have, over the past decade, shifted from equality of educational opportunity to instant equality of educational condition." [16] Robert Nisbet, the author of *The Degradation of the Academic Dogma,* joined in the onslaught on the City University's open admissions program with the usual white excuse that, "One cannot overnight erase the consequences of several hundred years' history," [17] and joined with Kristol in asserting that the university would graduate every student regardless of his academic attainment. With the utmost contempt for the teaching of writing, he asked, "Who of any quality would wish to teach in the program?" [18] An almost certain outcome of open admissions, said Nisbet, would be the deterioration of the liberal arts. Students entering a college under open admissions would flock, said he, to the "soft" disciplines: history, sociology, political science, and English, where, according to him, strict standards of excellence do not exist.[19] It would be impossible for open admissions students to graduate with B.A.s in such disciplines as mathematics, the physical sciences, economics, engineering, or psychology. Not one whit of empirical evidence did he introduce to support this thesis. Jacques Barzun, the former dean of Columbia, presided over these sessions, and predictably enough stated that "open admissions will be a *minority* [author's emphasis] privilege for which the entire country will be paying through various forms of taxation." [20] He went on to suggest that the best place for underachieving students would be the community colleges.[21] This from a man who characterized himself "as a greatly concerned individual, with compassion and concern for all people," and who, reluctantly, had to agree with Iriving Kristol's thoughts on open admissions.[22] The perception of open admissions by those scholars is representative of how deeply imbedded in the minds of many white professors is the fear of the erosion of standards implicit in the admissions of Black students onto their campuses, even when, as was the case in this instance, the fear of the entry of masses of Black students into the university was a mistaken image. Kenneth Clark aptly destroyed the Kristol, Barzun. and Nisbet theme that universities could not create academic miracles when he stated that "institutions, and particularly schools, do perform miracles. And one of the miracles which I think he [Kristol] is ignoring is the miracle of taking a precious human being and dehumanizing him. And it seems to me that this is a miracle that we accept. A kind of moral cynicism permits this miracle to continue when it actually could be remedied and solved, and I think those of us who believe that institutions are important in affecting the lives of human beings cannot permit ourselves to be seduced by your perspective. In fact, the more we hear of this perspective, the more we have to fight it." [23]

In the meantime, the University proceeded to the implementation of open admissions.

The allocation plan was obviously only a first step toward the accomplishment of this momentous educational experiment. But the parameters of the problem before the university were, in large measure, determined by the allocation system. The bulk of students in need of intensive remedial attention were in the community colleges and this, in turn, meant that a majority of those Black and Puerto Rican students with poor academic records were in two-year colleges. According to a university-wide test given on May 1, 1970, well over 50 per cent of the freshmen entering the community colleges were in need of compensatory education in both reading and mathematics. At some community and senior colleges, large percentages of the incoming students were in need of intensive reading and writing remediation; i.e., they had not attained a *ninth-grade achievement level* in either of these fields, despite the New York City Board of Education's requirement that all students graduating from high school in the city at least attain that level of competence.

The task, then, before the university was of unique proportions in educational history. It is no exaggeration to state that no institution of higher education in the world had ever set forth to give an opportunity for college graduation to such a large number of underprepared students. Some appreciation of the dimensions of the problem can be gained from the fact that the total number of SEEK students on all senior campuses in 1970 was 4,000 of a total student body of 119,000. Under open admissions, some 7,000 SEEK-like *freshmen* were to enter the city colleges yearly, while some community colleges' freshman classes were composed to a level of 50 per cent of students with high school averages below 70.

The SEEK program had always selected its students in random fashion, thus giving each college a broad spectrum of Black and Puerto Rican high school graduates with averages below those necessary for admission to the colleges. Therefore, proportionally few of these students had averages below 70. The community colleges of the system had likewise had little experience, particularly in the liberal arts transfer curriculum, with students below the 70 average. In short, the university, although pioneering in the education of students who did not meet regular standards of admission, had little experience in the education of large numbers who had failed to attain a 70 average in high school.

The consequent necessity for meticulous academic planning was evident. In order to anticipate the educational needs of the incoming freshmen, the university established a task force on open admissions in September 1969, long before the Board of Higher Education decided on the allocation system. The task force consisted of high-ranking central office executives who were to deal, individually, with every aspect of the open admissions problems: finances, space, admissions processing, faculty recruitment, and academic programming. I was given the task of developing academic guidelines for the treatment of O.A.P. students—i.e., those who would not have been admitted to the university under previous admissions criteria.

On everyone's mind was the immensity of the problem before us, and the possibility that some vital miscalculation, similar to Napoleon's failure to issue winter overcoats to his troops when he invaded Russia in 1812, would take place in the course of the planning process. Nowhere was this possibility more likely than in the area of academic planning. It should be noted, before explaining that process, that two vital decisions were

made in the fall of 1970 that laid down the ground rules for
the role of the task force in implementing open admissions. The
first decision, based on the premise that each college had a
personality of its own and on the fact that each college president must be made responsible for the success or failure of the
open admissions program on his campus, was to limit the task
force to suggesting plans of action for the colleges. The second
decision was to give the colleges unlimited flexibility in the
utilization of supplementary funds granted to the colleges for
the additional compensatory education and counseling activities
necessary to underpin the open admissions effort. The colleges
were to be required to submit plans of action, but unfortunately
there was to be no imposition onto the colleges of ironclad rules
of operation.

It was within the limitations imposed by these two decisions
that the academic planning for open admissions took place.
The academic guidelines, to which the colleges were to respond
with their own plans, were tightly constructed. The emphasis
in these guidelines was to ensure that the transition of O.A.P.
students from high school to college was accomplished in an
orderly and structured fashion. It was also assumed that it would
be necessary to create administrative devices that would pro-
tect underprepared students from that portion of the faculty
who felt that the entire program of open admissions constituted
an assault on the standards of the university. There is no
necessity for describing in detail the guidelines since they were
an exact replica of those I outlined in the chapter on compensatory education.

The primary aim of the issuance of the guidelines in the fall
of 1969 was to elicit concrete plans of action from each of the
colleges. Each of these institutions had created its own task
forces on open admissions and appointed a coordinator of the
open admissions effort. By March 1970, each college, in fact,
had prepared a plan of action or nonaction for its compensatory
education program. The variations in the approaches to the problem were so wide as to represent a microcosm of compensatory
education programs throughout the country.

The actual plans of each college reflected varying internal

pressures and faculty and administrative priorities. Therefore, some colleges moved to beef up their entire freshman counseling, orientation, and registration procedures, on the assumption that O.A.P. students would be offended were they singled out for special treatment. Other colleges, rather than create special compensatory sections, decided to create elaborate tutorial arrangements for students whom instructors found in need of such attention. Still others, while maintaining the regular structure, decided that remediation instruction would be given in an additional fourth-hour session to be added to a regularly scheduled three-hour course. Some colleges decided that incoming freshmen lacking the traditional number of high school units would be required to complete those missing courses on a non-credit basis.

The same diversity was evident in the arrangements for counseling, with some colleges opting for regular faculty members to serve as advisers to incoming freshmen, others depending on traditional student counseling departments, and still others relying on specially recruited counselors to work with the new freshmen.

Each of the plans submitted by the colleges was subjected to a critique by the central task force on open admissions, and then the colleges were left free to make whatever adjustments in their plans they felt necessary in light of the suggestions for changes made by the central office. This was a major blunder on the part of the central university administration.

The primary method of dealing with the diversity of approaches prevalent in the university was the dispatching to the colleges of teams of evaluators from the office of the Vice-Chancellor of Academic Affairs. These teams meticulously examined every aspect of the O.A.P. at each college, interviewed faculty, deans, registrars, and students, and, in addition, scrutinized transcripts of O.A.P. students to ascertain the actual results of the orientation, placement, and registration procedures recommended by the central task force on open admissions. Written reports on the results of the evaluations were sent to each college with recommendations for changes in procedures found faulty,

In the interests of preventing other universities from repeating those mistakes made in the first year of the open admissions experiment, some general observations on their nature
will be made here. First, it was clear that the most common
difficulty was that of placing students into courses commen-
surate with their reading, writing, and mathematics achievement levels. Even when—and this was not always the case—
students had been placed into compensatory courses and into
supposedly low-level freshman courses, it often turned out that
the students, during the process of registration, would find that
the courses they had been counseled to enter were full. This resulted in their taking substitute courses for which they were not
prepared academically. In other instances, colleges had not prepared a full complement of courses for students who were
totally unready for regular course work. Counseling procedures,
moreover, were frequently premised on voluntary requests by
underprepared students for such services. The colleges soon
found that the students most in need of counseling never appeared. Tutorial sessions, well worked out on paper, became en-
tangled in scheduling difficulties between student tutors and
underprepared students. Thus, a multitude of foreseen and unforeseen difficulties plagued the first year of the open admissions
program.

On the other hand, exciting and innovative approaches to'
the problem of compensatory education appeared throughout
the university. At one college, a programmed audiovisual approach to college algebra with branches leading the student back
to those mathematical concepts he missed in high school proved
highly successful, even with students who entered the college
with ninth-grade mathematical achievement levels. At another,
a writing laboratory with structured exercises specifically geared
toward the deficiencies of O.A.P. students operated on a twelve-
hour-a-day basis. Students were able to receive immediate di-
agnosis and feedback on their writing difficulties. Throughout
the university, then, there were pockets of innovation that
promised, in time, to develop methods of instruction that could
be used on a large-scale basis to deal with the specific needs of
the university's new population.

To correct the problem areas detected by the monitoring teams from the central office, the Vice-Chancellor for Academic Affairs, in June 1971, issued a memorandum detailing both the areas of difficulty and proposed solutions:

1. *Problem*—Students are puzzled, confused, and at times frightened by their initial contact with the collegiate world.
   Recommendation—Each college should develop a mandatory orientation program for freshmen to take place prior to registration, and preferably as soon as possible after the student has been notified of his acceptance by the university. The orientation can familiarize the student with the college, make clear the placement procedures it has worked out for compensatory courses, and give him some grasp of the rationale of these courses.
2. *Problem*—The generalized placement tests which the university itself administers aren't detailed or precise enough for the individual college placement operation.
   Recommendation—Each college should administer a battery of placement tests to assess the specific academic needs of each freshman. These tests must be given at an early enough date to permit scheduling by the registrar of an adequate number of freshman courses for the fall semester. The minimum areas in which testing should be given are reading skills, written English, and mathematics. Individual colleges may feel they want further measures, and these could of course be included in the battery.
3. *Problem*—Too many students are entering courses for which they are partially or totally unprepared.
   Recommendation—When a student's placement examination indicates inability to function at the normal freshman level either in individual subject areas or across the board, his entire program must be approved in writing by a duly authorized faculty member. The coordinator of open admissions on the campus can make certain that this is done.
4. *Problem*—Students who are given adequate advice find at the time of actual registration that the courses they were advised to enter are closed out.
   Recommendation—The college shall make its registrar responsible for providing enough places in its courses to ensure that students are actually placed in the course program which has been approved by their faculty adviser. It may be necessary for the college to give the coordinator of open admissions authority to override both registrar and departmental chairman if this should be necessary.

5. *Problem*—Several colleges have not instituted developmental courses, and the results have been disastrous.

   Recommendation—Each college shall institute courses in developmental reading and study skills, basic written English, and developmental mathematics. It is very strongly recommended that no more than 15 students be placed in a section of any such course. Whether or not the college wishes to give credit for those parts of such courses which include college level work should be left to the discretion of the individual college.

6. *Problem*—There is considerable confusion as to who should take or who can profit from remedial and developmental courses.

   Recommendation—The following general criteria should govern the placement of freshmen:

   a) Students whose *high school records and placement test scores* indicate ability to take a regular full freshman course load shall be permitted to do so.

   b) Students in need of limited developmental work may be enrolled in some "regular" courses, but their program must be limited to 12 to 13 credits or combined credits and hours.

   c) Students in need of intense developmental work, *as a rule,* should not be enrolled in regular college courses until such time as their academic readiness for such courses is evident. Instead, the colleges shall develop either stretched-out sequences of introductory courses or special preparatory social science and science courses for such students. Such courses, *in no case,* shall be developed beyond the introductory level of any discipline.

   d) Each college shall devise a grading system for compensatory instruction that recognizes its preparatory nature. Stringent attendance regulations shall obtain in all compensatory courses. No student, however, shall be dropped for academic reasons before the end of one full year of attendance.

   e) The above-listed criteria should not be construed as binding upon the college in all cases. Exceptions to such placements, however, may only be accomplished through the written approval of a duly authorized faculty member.

7. *Problem*—The essential point of difficulty for freshmen with inadequate preparation is the "switch point" when they are integrated into the college. In almost every college there is some confusion, and in several colleges this confusion was considerable.

   Recommendation—Each college shall assign a full-tme counselor to each 50 to 75 freshman students who have been placed in two or more developmental skills courses.

Inspections of the colleges in the fall of 1971 indicated that most of them had taken steps to shore up the weak points, but by this time indications were forthcoming that the major threat to open admissions did not lie in the academic structure of the program, but in the stringent New York state and city budget cutbacks that threatened to make impossible the concentrated attention on underprepared students necessary to give them a fair chance for academic success.

The Black and Puerto Rican students who began the uprising that led to the open admissions program have long since either graduated or left school to turn their attention to community work. The three faculty members most influential in bringing about this momentous educational change—Betty Rawls and Alfred Conrad of CCNY, and Lloyd Delaney of Queens—are deceased, all at a young age. But their legacies are such as to have shaken the entire academic establishment of the country. I do not know, as of this writing, whether open admissions will be a success or not. However, it has opened vistas for Black and Puerto Rican high school youth previously condemned to a life of poverty because their averages and S.A.T. scores did not meet the requirements of the City University of New York. And, whether they like it or not, no public institution of higher learning in this country will ever be able to fall back to its traditional posture of writing off Black youth as "uneducable" because of poor performances in deteriorating high schools. College admissions policies may not all take the form of the City University's experiment, but they will never be the same again.

Whither Black Education?

The history of the Black struggle for higher education is punctuated by the basic complacency of the white university, the early effort by Black educators to develop strategies for higher education within a segregated context, and, finally, the inevitable clash that took place once white institutions decided to educate Black youth. The history and the tumult has only begun. It was reported in a recent newspaper article that a white educator, with no higher degree than an M.A., had been chosen to preside over a community college whose racial composition is over 60 per cent Black and Puerto Rican. Actions like this will make further clashes inevitable, until whites get the message that the Black people of this country wish to control their own educational destinies in those institutions that are—by virtue of white policy—predominantly Black.

The problems of educating Black youth in higher education have changed very little over the years. David Walker argued that the mere thought of educating Blacks struck terror into the hearts of the oppressors, a phenomenon that can be observed when some white administrators falsely blame all their troubles on campus on the regularly admitted Black middle-class students, not on the underprepared, economically poor Blacks recruited under E.O.P. programs. There is still a gap between the educational levels of Blacks and whites. Education remains the primary lever by which the racial situation in this country can be controlled and changed—not simply at the college level, but also in high schools, elementary schools, and day-care centers, where today hundreds of thousands of Black youth are being separated from the elemental knowledge necessary for them to compete equally with whites when they become adults.

Many paradoxes and contradictions have emerged so far in our discussion of the Black population's search for higher educational opportunities in a society dominated by whites. The fact of segregation and the unwillingness of white faculties to accept Black scholars as colleagues resulted in an outpouring of Black historical and sociological research in the 1920s and '30s, ironically surpassing in scope and productivity the work of contemporary Black scholars scattered over innumerable white campuses. A contradiction surely exists between the integrationist demand that Black students be admitted to previously all-white campuses and the separatist demand that students be treated differently once they arrive on the campus. There is the further paradox that although the traditional liberal arts curriculum has been challenged by Blacks, it does contain a core of knowledge necessary for a multifaceted view of the world, which is of immense value to the Black student searching for new ways to approach the problems of his own people. In fact, within the entire spectrum of Black studies programs one finds paradoxes. Few Afro-Americans are properly equipped to teach the courses, and if one probes deeply into the subject, one finds one must use references from white scholarly sources. There are no easy answers to any of these questions and, as in most historical periods of change, there will be many false starts and failures before the necessary synthesis is evolved.

At the core of these contradictions lies the unresolved dilemma within the Black community: whether to fight for integration or separation. The ideological struggle between these two opposing forces is essentially wasteful of the intellectual energy necessary to deal with the more basic question of the actual survival of Black people in this country. When one considers even for a moment the genocidal possibilities that might result, for example, from a Black assassina·ing a president of the United States, the battle of words among separatists and integrationists becomes a relatively meaningless academic exercise. To pit the concept of integration against that of separation is to set up a battle of straw men. Obviously, there are innumerable permutations and combinations of the two strategies, and the particular question to be asked in any situation is whether the stance taken is beneficial to Black people. Assuming that 10 per cent of a white college's population is composed of Black E.O.P. students, then it makes sense that at one and the same time Blacks can demand special separatist compensatory educational structures for the students while pushing for the placement of Blacks in positions of real power in the college. In political analogy, one can support at the same time the election of more Black legislative officials to white assemblies and the creation by those elected of their own Black caucuses.

Certain minimal guidelines might shed more light on the directions in which Black people should move, based on a realistic assessment of the actual state of Black people in this country today. Data from the census of 1970 give us an approximation of that condition.[1]

Black people make up 11 per cent of the total population of the country, with only 53 per cent of that number remaining in the South. In the northern part of America, over three-quarters of Blacks are located in the central cities. Within the past two decades, there have been significant shifts in the Black population of major cities, both Southern and Northern. During that time, Blacks in New York have risen from 10 to 21 per cent of the city's population. Comparable figures for Chicago, Baltimore, Washington, and Cleveland are 14–33 per cent, 24–46 per cent, 35–71 per cent, and 16–38 per cent.

The median income of Black people in this country remains far below that of whites, having risen from a point of 54 per cent in 1950, to 64 per cent in 1970. Only 16 per cent of Blacks earn between $10,000 and $15,000 a year, while 28 per cent of whites are in this category. At the other end of the scale, 20 per cent of all Blacks have a yearly income below $3,000, while only 8 per cent of whites find themselves in such a desperate economic plight. In this country, Black men with high school diplomas earn less than whites with only eight years of schooling. And a Black man, having finished college, will still only earn 70 per cent of the salary of a white college graduate. Unemployment among Blacks is twice that of whites, while among Black teen-agers, the rate of unemployment is 30 per cent, as opposed to the 13.5 per cent figure for white teen-agers. Black workers compose only 5 per cent of the total union membership in crafts and trades unions, and the probability is that their numbers are below one per cent in many of the specialized unions.

In education, the Black dropout rate in high school was 15.9 per cent as contrasted with 6.7 per cent for whites, and only 5.8 per cent of Black males between the ages of 25 and 34 had completed four years of college, while the comparable rate for whites was 20.9 per cent. Finally, the infant mortality rate for Black babies during the first year of life remains three times as great as that for white babies.

These statistics give but the bare skeleton of the condition of the Black population in America today. As in the case with all sets of numbers—"the death of one man is a tragedy, the death of ten thousand a statistic"—they conceal the physical condition of housing, the dehumanization in welfare centers and under-manned clinics, the narcotics infestation destroying thousands of Black youth, the inability of many Black students, upon completion of high school, to do simple arithmetic calculations, or the psychic and physical toll implicit in merely surviving in the central-city environments.

Now, no one today questions the roots of these conditions— they are planted deep in both the historical and contemporary racism of American society. This phenomenon manifests itself in personal, economic, educational, and social decisions made daily by a multiplicity of white institutions. Bankers deciding on where to invest their funds for housing, television producers and newspaper editors deciding on policy toward Black people, and politicians on every level of government who in budgeting decide who gets what are all involved in that matrix of white power that inevitably has its impact on the fate of Black people. Foundations, in the twinkling of an eye, can decide which Black colleges are to survive and which are to be eliminated. The governor of the state of New York, with a simple signature, can and has cut by one-quarter the allocations of food to Black families living under the poverty level. Furthermore, the income of the vast

majority of Black Americans today is dependent upon employment within the white economy.

The overwhelming dependency of the Black population upon
the white economy and the relative powerlessness of the Afro-
American to change that relationship—through guns, political
maneuverings, or welfare protest groups—keeps us from finding
the answer to the problems that beset Black Americans. Integrationists continue to argue with separatists; community control frequently degenerates into clashes between the Black
middle-class "poverty workers" and the poor they are supposed to
serve; and Pan-Africanists refuse to accept the solutions proposed by the Black Panthers.

And, in the meantime, educational genocide continues. White
teachers' unions have destroyed promising educational experiments, such as the I.E. 201 complex in Harlem. The Head Start
Program has become of little concern to the federal government,
and hundreds of thousands of Black youth in school systems
throughout the country are falling behind in their reading and
arithmetic skills. A relevant step toward alleviating the educational and social conditions of Black people and toward eventual
Black control over the mechanisms dominating their lives would
be the creation of skilled cadres, ideologically committed to the
upgrading of the levels of academic competence of Black youth
in particular, and intent upon improving the life of the Black
community in general. We must set our sights high and create
over the next decade trained Blacks who, in every category of
the professions, will be proportionate in number to whites in
those professions.

One can proceed from this base to the construction of a Black
strategy for higher education. We must first, in methodical
fashion, increase the proportion of Black undergraduates in all
four-year institutions to 25 per cent. This should be the first and
foremost goal. It follows that Black educators should begin to
measure the potential of Black youth so that we may develop our
own criteria as to which Black youth should enter which institutions. One cannot avoid the fact that Harvard has a better
physics department than Westchester State Teachers' College.
Criteria must be developed to channel Black students—from all
strata of the Black community—to those better institutions

where they will become most useful to Black society. We need Black atomic physicists as badly as we need Black school-teachers.

The initial thrust should be toward the four-year colleges, because in reality—confirmed by reports and recommendations from the Carnegie Corporation and present federal policy—the majority of Black youth is being channeled into two-year community colleges. This movement can only be counteracted by strong insistence by the Black community that our youth be placed in four-year institutions. Some Black youth do belong in community colleges, since they do not have the potential for a four-year degree and can profit from some of the technical skills taught in the community colleges. Many whites belong there too, but the national movement to place the majority of Black youth into such institutions effectively maintains the educational differential between Blacks and whites. When junior colleges are all Black, as they are presently in many urban areas, then the Black community should demand that the leadership of those institutions also be Black.

The next educational target should be the graduate schools of this country. Through them we can begin to produce the large numbers of Black scholars and professionals needed to counteract the white monopoly on the professions. The same quota of 25 per cent should be demanded of those graduate schools which, if anything, are more conservative in their feelings of obligation to the Black community than the undergraduate colleges of the country. Nothing is more indicative of this fact than a report prepared for the Carnegie Foundation by Bernard Berelson, a professor at Columbia, which in all of its three hundred pages on the status of graduate education omitted any reference to the necessity for these institutions to address themselves to the needs of the Black population.

The Black community, as it devises and refines plans for the higher education of its youth, should be acutely aware of those white institutional structures that serve as the chief influences on educational policy and determine the priorities of the allocation of resources to higher education. The major foundations, the associations of university presidents, the National Science Foundation, the U.S. Office of Education, and the National Academy of Sciences are all dominated by whites who apparently feel free to decide what educational policies are in the best interests of Black people with little or no Black input into those decisions. I can scarcely forget one encounter with a white program officer of a foundation. When presented with an innovative proposal for the teaching of mathematics to Black students, this man told me that the proposal would be scrutinized by an advisory group of the "best minds" in the country. In enumerating the composition of this body, it turned out that not one of these persons was Black, nor did any of them have even a nodding acquaintance with the educational problems of Black children. There must be constant, unremitting pressure on these controlling institutions—even if it takes the extreme form of refusing their grants—demanding substantial Black influence upon decisions that affect Black people, particularly Black youth.

A further difficult and controversial question related to Black education concerns the role of the Black scholar, in a Black studies program or in a regular college department. Du Bois stands almost alone as an example of the Black scholar engagé. One can only admire his awesome capacity for blending excellence of scholarship with constant political activity. Unfortunately, few are endowed by nature with either his immense vitality or his enormous capacity for concentration on the task at hand.

At this juncture in history, the first priority of Black scholars should be the creation of a body of knowledge and theory to serve the Black movement. Today we can contrast the enormous scholarly productivity of the faculties of Atlanta, Fisk, and Howard universities three decades ago with the relative scarcity of contemporary Black scholarship. This condition has deep-seated causes, the most important of which is the tendency of the federal government and the foundations to bestow millions of dollars in research funds upon white specialists in Black affairs. Another cause is the integration of white universities' faculties and the consequent diffusion of Black scholars across the country. The intellectual cross-fertilization which fostered the early Black scholars' creative work has disappeared, a direct result of integration. Those Black scholars—and they are substantial both in numbers and in the quality of their work—who do publish, frequently have their work ignored while white America turns to men like Coleman, Moynihan, and Jencks for policy guidance toward Black people. Black scholars, then, must exert themselves even further to put forth their ideas and works to preempt white incursions into the affairs of Black people. If, in fact, there are to be changes in the educational structures to solve the problem of young Black dropouts, then the answers must come from Black scholars. In the same vein, the creation of new curricula for students in predominantly Black systems should be the object of Black scholarly attention. If the Black community is to create viable institutions of its own, then Black scholarship will have to begin in-depth studies of white society and the relationships between its political, economic, and social mechanisms and the Black condition.

The aim here would be to dissect these institutions in order to pinpoint targets for Black strategy during the 1970s. It is not enough to know that the banking system of America discriminates against Blacks in the distribution of loans, mortgages, and investments. The Black community must know precisely and in detail the various devices and policy-making bodies utilized for this purpose. In a study of the American political system at all levels, general contours and viable tactics for counterpoising its oppressive effect must be outlined. Such studies can only emanate from the finest and best-trained minds that the Black community possesses. Those capable of such analysis should not feel constricted in their research to abide by any ideology other than the primary one of exploring, in depth, viable alternatives for Black people in this society. If the scholar decides to abhor all political activity in pursuit of this end, then that should be his business. In the last years of his life, having seen the repeated failures of revolutionary efforts, Karl Marx effectively excluded himself from political activities and buried himself in the British Museum to try to discover why the revolutions had failed and how future revolutions could succeed. From his lonely years of research emerged *Das Kapital,* the work that provided the ideological base for the remaking of half of the world.

Some Black scholars will choose to concentrate on research, but that does not mean that others should not serve in all levels of activity in the Black community. Thus, the Congressional Black caucus should not have to expend its monies hiring a research staff, when there exist Black scholars in every field who can and should provide a permanent pool of experts for the caucus, writing position papers on questions concerning the Black community. Such scholars are scattered throughout the country and should perform such services for Black politicians on every level. If Arthur Schlesinger, Jr., John Galbraith, and other scholars provide "brain trusts" for white politicians, then it is incumbent upon Black scholars to do likewise without any remuneration other than the satisfaction that they are advancing the empowerment of Black people. The same type of technical expertise should be available for the entire range of Black community organizations. Nor is this to suggest that some scholars—the best example is George Wiley, leader of the Welfare Rights Movement—should not opt for direct participation in the movement . . . "Let a hundred flowers bloom."

In white institutions of higher education, Black professors must demand both from the universities and from the students the best education possible. Students should be encouraged to use all the educational resources of the institution, to take a broad range of offerings, and not to be forced into any one ideologically constricted path to learning. Moreover, Black students should be counseled not to follow in the tracks of the bored white dropouts with 700 S.A.T. scores, who, whether they finish college or not, are intellectually prepared for any number of technical or managerial positions when they decide to return to the "system," an option hardly accessible to underprepared Black youth. Most important to the successful destruction of the educational gap between whites and Blacks is the inculcation into the minds of Black youth of today and tomorrow of a hierarchy of values, at the top of which stands a positive attitude toward intellectualism. Ideological blindfolds might, for example, make a Black student unwilling to take a course in the history of Zionism and the creation of the state of Israel. He would thereby be robbed of an exciting and instructive case study in a variety of developmental techniques, both nationally and internationally based, which created the strongest industrial and military state in the Middle East.

On the other hand, Black professors on white campuses must constantly emphasize the necessity for attention to the specific needs of Black students. They must receive the academic counseling and financial support necessary to complete college. This means that the Black faculty must constantly be on the alert for the innumerable administrative ploys on the part of colleges, diluting the resources available to these students. There should be an awareness that Black students in white colleges have different cultural and social needs from their white classmates. While the recognition of this "specialness" of cultural needs may frequently lead to aberrations—i.e., the beating of bongo drums all night long in a Black dormitory—one can expect that with time these dormitories and cultural centers will become places where the young Black intelligentsia will begin educating themselves, engaging in serious discourses about the Black condition. One can also predict that white colleges will soon accept this Black separatism with the same spirit that they accepted, in the past, fraternities, clubs, and special houses on campus.

There must be a further search for educational alternatives to the present system. I have already suggested the creation of urban Black colleges as one alternative. Others come to mind. If some Black youth find white Northern campuses intolerable, then why not explore the alternatives of a voucher system that would permit them to enter Southern Black colleges—where the environment might be more conducive to their psychic, academic, and social growth—thus providing at the same time a supply of students and monies to these financially weakened institutions. Various compensatory education programs around the country have indicated that within a year they can raise a student's reading level by three years and teach him to write on a college freshman level. If such effects can be achieved within a year with students who graduated from high school with reading levels at the tenth grade, then the possibility of eliminating the last year of high school for underprepared Black students and admitting them to college compensatory programs at the end of their junior year should be explored. Such a project would eliminate the waste of one more year's lockstep in the high school system and serve as a strong stimulus for Black high school students to remain in school.

We must always be sure to "hold on to what we've got." What Black people do have is a network of Black colleges in the South, public and private, that are in danger of extinction by integration. A report on the thirty-five previously all-Black public colleges in the country indicates that three institutions—West Virginia State College, Bluefield State College (West Virginia), and Lincoln University (Missouri)—now have a majority of white students.[2] Three other colleges—Delaware State, Bowie State (Maryland), and Kentucky State—have white enrollments of over 30 per cent. Another three schools—Maryland State, Prairie View A & M (Texas), and Arkansas A & M—have been absorbed by larger and older predominantly white state institutions. In addition, fourteen of the remaining colleges are facing increasing competition for students from white Southern community and four-year colleges in close proximity to them. The same fate seems imminent for the fifty-four Black private colleges in the South which, deprived for the most part of state and federal monies, are in great financial difficulty. In October 1971, the Ford Foundation announced a grant of $100 million to strengthen Black colleges, but most of these monies will be given to only ten of the fifty-four institutions. The foundation is, in effect, writing off as unsalvageable the remaining private Black institutions.

These colleges, with their long-standing commitment to Black students and their experience in coping with the severe educational deficiencies of Black youth, may be eliminated. The consequences for Black higher education, both in terms of the special educational needs of Black students and the coming dispersion of Black professors into integrated institutions, will probably be disastrous. Yet, aside from the association of Black presidents created three years ago, there seems to be little pressure emanating from the Black community to preserve such colleges as institutions where total attention can be paid to Black students.

A prerequisite for the creation of a Black higher education agenda is the organization of a strong national body of Black scholars of *all* political hues and all disciplines to serve as a political and intellectual lobby to advance the cause of the education of Black youth. It would need a strong central staff and a journal that focused exclusively on the educational problem of Blacks in America. The foundations have long seen fit to fund whites interested in studying these problems, but—with some exceptions—they seem to draw the line at extending similar sums of money to Black educators interested in solving the problems of the education of Black youth.

One comes now to the final question: What can white institutions do to assure educational justice to the Black youth who will, in increasing numbers, be entering freshman classes? The historical and contemporary record of these institutions has largely been one of maintaining the racial status quo. White academics cling with a tenacity to the racial stereotypes of the society. Time after time, by their writings or their actions, they revert to the theme of the genetic mental inferiority of Black people. The general reaction of today's white colleges to the entrance of Black students onto their campuses reflects that bias. Parochial and inward-looking, these colleges have made little progress toward understanding the simple truth that unless they compensate for long years of neglect, they are on a path leading directly to the dissolution of both the colleges and society as a whole. Even less have the universities embraced the role of transmitting values to their white students that will permit them to build a country freed of the racial inequities that now plague it. Indeed, most institutions have absorbed the Black students' initial thrust for change by creating "autonomous" E.O.P. and ethnic studies programs. Yet few colleges have moved beyond that point to a true empowerment of Blacks within white institutions. Power over the control of monies, personnel, and curricula still rests in the hands of assorted white deans, departmental chairmen, and faculty committees. White colleges have made little effort to put Blacks into such "regular" positions. Moreover, the content of the traditional curriculum still reflects an almost totally white view of America. Schools of education continue to be dominated by whites and to produce persons unable to cope with the problems of urban schools. Swarms of white professors, despite the obvious resistance of the Black community, continue to probe that community with research

studies that ultimately provide the basis for governmental policies toward Black people. White academia, having done what the
Black students asked, goes on its merry way.

Now, this state of affairs may well remain undisturbed at
campuses that have only a small proportion of Blacks in their
total student bodies. But it is an invitation to disaster in major
public urban four-year and two-year colleges that will be receiv-
ing Black students in ever larger increments. The existence of
the tenure system and the reluctance of whites to give up administrative posts that are not vested with tenure can only lead
to major confrontations between the colleges, Black students,
and the Black communities that will increasingly surround these
colleges. The outcome will almost certainly be disruptions of
the type that have accompanied the changes in student-body
composition of urban high schools throughout the country.

If white colleges wish to bring about some type of coexistence
on campuses, their first and foremost act should be a recognition
of the institutionalized racism built into their structures. No
necessity exists for self-flagellation in this matter, just a calm
and rational appraisal of the college and its inbred attitude toward Black people. The search might begin in the library. How
many volumes in its catalogue deal with the Black question?
How many of its total professional staff are Black? Are there
any Black administrators in the library? One might turn to the
registrar's office and subject it to the same type of scrutiny. In-
vading the sanctity of academic freedom, the college might col-
lect, without instructors' names, syllabi in the social sciences
and humanities and scrutinize them for the incidence of Black
works appearing in them. A president might well wish to evalu-
ate the percentage of Blacks among the chief line officers of the
college—excluding, of course, the various Blacks bearing titles
related to "minority affairs," "ethnic affairs," or "urban affairs."
The inevitable result of such a survey will indicate the steps
to be taken by a college before Black students can have any
sense that the college has an institutional commitment to racial
equality.

White faculty and staff need reorientation toward the special
needs of the new population of students entering their institutions. Given the innate conservatism of most faculty and their

reluctance to adapt to changing conditions, there will be an outcry against such a training program. But most colleges are going to have little choice in this matter: either they anticipate the problems that will occur between Black students and white faculty and move, in positive fashion, to reorient the faculty, or the students themselves will retrain the faculty—and not necessarily in a manner conducive to a learning atmosphere.

College presidents, most of all, must begin to examine their own personal commitment to equal opportunity in education. It is easy enough to react negatively to every suggestion calling for new curricula and ways of dealing with new students. Those in history who have foreseen the necessity for change and acted so as to channel those changes constructively stand out as great leaders, while the negativists and obstructionists have inevitably been placed in the "ashpit of history."

Self-examination cannot be restricted to the level of college presidents. Professional associations of scholars, foundations, educational executives ensconced in the various agencies should also scrutinize their attitudes. The purpose of such examination, it should be emphasized, is in their own best interests, if they do, in fact, desire a society free of the clashes and violence dominating the past decade.

It is also incumbent upon all white institutions concerned with higher education to recognize that the Black community is determined to build its own organizations and control its own destiny. The thrust will not stop three, five, or twenty years from now. And in this context, white researchers, white urban specialists, white schools of education, and white "think tanks" must understand that their primary function will be that of "being on tap, not on top." If that one simple thought would penetrate into the entire white educational structure, one small step would be taken toward a peaceful coexistence in this country between Blacks and whites.

My own feeling about the ability or willingness of white institutions to change in a positive fashion is pessimistic. Having a knowledge of E.O.P. programs around the country and having seen the academic elimination of almost 75 per cent of the students in certain programs within a year, I am unconvinced of the will of most colleges to redress the educational imbalance existing between whites and Blacks. The pessimism is daily shored up by news like the public statement by a white president of a major college that his major concern in taking office was the opportunity to expand the Black enrollment at his institution—privately, and in writing, however, he made every effort to minimize the number of Black students on his campus. At other institutions, monies allocated for poor Black students have been diverted to aid lower-middle-income white students. Certain presidents and deans, having admitted underprepared Black students to their colleges, have turned their faces away from the programs until the academic slaughter has occurred, only to say, "This really proves we should never have taken them in in the first place."

In the face of such attitudes—and they are prevalent across the country—the messages of Woodson and Du Bois about the creation of Black universities take on greater strength and vitality day by day. If, as it seems, underprepared Black students are condemned to academic extermination in white institutions and if, as I have daily witnessed, a vast intellectual potential rests in the minds of those Black students, then the Black community has no other alternative than to establish a network of Black colleges specifically geared toward the education of those students. One cannot wait on the sidelines, while year after year Black students are delivered to the tender mercies of white academicians with very little commitment to the intellectual development of these students. Certainly these white institutions may change over the years, but the stakes are too great for the Black community to wait until that gradual change takes place. In the face of a technological revolution that will soon surpass the Industrial Revolution in its impact on the social, economic, and political aspects of human life, Black people can scarcely afford to wait "one more time" for American society to act in a manner consistent with its self-proclaimed role as the world's greatest democracy. We've been there before.

Notes

Quotation in front of book: Greenwich, Conn.: Fawcett Publications, 1969, p. 70.

CHAPTER 2

1. David Walker, "Attack upon Abjectness and Ignorance," reprinted in *The Negro Caravan,* ed. by Sterling A. Brown, Arthur P. Davis, and Ulysses Lee (Arno Press and the New York Times, 1961), pp. 588–94.
2. Ibid., p. 594.
3. W. E. B. Du Bois, *Autobiography of W. E. B. Du Bois* (New York: International Publications, 1968), p. 312.
4. Winthrop D. Jordan, *White Over Black* (Chapel Hill, N.C.: University of North Carolina Press, 1968).
5. Ibid., p. 187.
6. George M. Fredrickson, *The Black Image in the White Mind* (New York: Harper & Row, 1971), p. 51.
7. Jordan, op. cit., p. 437.
8. Henry Allen Bullock, *A History of Negro Education in the South* (Cambridge, Mass.: Harvard University Press, 1967), p. 93.
9. Ibid., p. 123.
10. Ibid., p. 76.
11. August Meier, *Negro Thought in America: 1880–1915* (Ann Arbor: University of Michigan Press, 1963), p. 88.
12. James M. McPherson, "White Liberals and Black Power in Negro Education: 1865–1915," *American Historical Review* 15 (June 1970): 1357–86.
13. Jordan, op. cit., p. 554.
14. Bullock, op. cit., p. 42.
15. Christopher Jencks and David Riesman, *The Academic Revolution* (Garden City, N.Y.: Doubleday and Co., Inc., 1968), p. 406. For documentation see Harvey Wish, "American Slave Insurrection Before 1861," *Journal of Negro History* XXII (July 1932): 229–320; and Raymond A. Bauer and Alice H. Bauer, "Day to Day Resistance

to Slavery," *Journal of Negro History* XXVII (October 1942): 338–419.

16. *Negro Social and Political Thought,* ed. by Howard Brotz (New York: Basic Books, 1966), pp. 224–25.

17. Ibid., p. 351.

18. Du Bois, op. cit., p. 203.

19. Ibid., p. 312.

20. *W. E. B. Du Bois: A Reader,* ed. by Meyer Weinberg (New York: Harper & Row, 1970), "The Negro College," pp. 177–88.

21. Washington, D.C.: Associated Publishers, 1933.

22. Ibid., p. xii.

23. Op. cit.

24. Ibid., p. 426.

CHAPTER 3

1. Clark Kerr, *The Uses of the University* (Cambridge, Mass.: Harvard University Press, 1964), p. 45.

2. Ibid., p. 87.

3. James Ridgeway, *The Closed Corporation: American Universities in Crisis* (New York: Random House, 1968).

4. Robert Nisbet, *The Degradation of the Academic Dogma* (New York: Basic Books, 1971).

5. Ridgeway, op. cit., passim.

6. Bernard Berelson, *Graduate Education in the United States* (New York: McGraw Hill, 1960), pp. 132–37.

7. James Allen Moss, "Negro Teachers in Predominantly White Colleges," *Journal of Negro Education* XXVII (Fall 1958): 451–62. A Black, Father Patrick Francis Healy, S.J., was the president of Georgetown University from 1873 to 1882. Dr. George Grant was made an instructor at Harvard's School of Dentistry in 1884. William H. Hinton was an instructor at Harvard Medical School from 1915 to 1949. In 1949, the year before his retirement, he became a professor.

8. Fred G. Wale, "Chosen for Ability," *Atlantic Monthly,* July 1947: 87.

9. A survey of 1,000 Northern institutions in 1948 revealed a grand total of 133 Black professors in these colleges. R. B. Atwood, H. S. Smith, and Catherine V. Vaughn, "Negro Teachers in Northern Colleges and Universities in the United States," *Journal of Negro Education* XVIII (Fall 1949): 564–67.

10. Moss, op. cit., p. 451.

11. In the interest of a fairness which was never extended to Blacks by the earlier writings of these persons, it should be noted that Odum and many others cited in this section did change their views on racial matters over the years. Thus, for example, Robert

Penn Warren did denounce, in subsequent years, his contribution to *I'll Take My Stand.* The tenth edition of Ogg and Ray's *Essentials of American National Government,* re-edited by William H. Young, 1969, eliminates the offending references to the Black question. The 1970 edition of Ferguson and McHenry devotes 9 pages of 528 to the status of Blacks in America, but still states, on page 110, that anti-Black laws "were prompted not only by deep-seated prejudices and concepts of racial superiority carried over from the slavery era, but also *by excesses of the reconstruction period*" (emphasis mine). The sixth edition of Carr, Bernstein, Murphy, and Danielson, *American Democracy 1971,* removes the reference to "extremists," and places considerable emphasis on the Black status in this country. The chapter on the Constitution still bears no reference to the inapplicability of that document to Blacks, but a full chapter of 21 pages has been added on the Black question out of a total of 571 pages. There are also scattered references throughout the book on Blacks. The 1972 eighth edition version of Burns and Peltason contains a full chapter of some 30 pages on the same matter out of 526 pages dealing with national government, and contains scattered references throughout the book to Blacks. Thus, some change has occurred, but I would like to emphasize that the earlier versions of their works were chosen specifically to illustrate the prevailing academic approach to the Black question in the period prior to 1960 because it was in this environment that most of today's leaders and academicians received their education.

12. Lloyd Marcus, *The Treatment of Minorities in Secondary School Textbooks* (Anti-Defamation League of B'nai B'rith: 1961), p. 38. An even more recent and thorough survey by Marc Krug in the *School Review* ("Freedom of Racial Equality: A study of 'Revised' High School texts," LXXXVIII [May 1970]: 297–352) centered itself on the fashion in which high school textbooks "revised" after the Black agitation of the 1960s had changed in their treatment of several major historical issues, such as the Civil War, slavery, Reconstruction, and the 1954 Supreme Court school desegregation decision. Krug was searching in these books for (p. 301) "an open commitment to the basic fundamental values of human freedom . . . and a forthright antipathy to the crimes committed by the white community against the Blacks in the course of our history." He concluded that there had been an improvement in the textbook's approach to the subject of Blacks, but that there was still a need for *"major improvements and major revisions"* (p. 347, emphasis his). These included the necessity for textbook writers to stop the glossing-over and equivocation about slavery, the need to tell fully the story of the Black Abolitionists, a rejection of the old myths about Reconstruction, a concentration on "the struggles of *Blacks for their own freedom,*" and a discarding of the "impression

. . . that all the fighting for Black freedom and equality was done by the *whites for the Blacks"* (p. 348, emphasis his).

13. New York: Harper & Brothers, 1907.

14. As quoted, p. 684, in Michael R. Winston: "Through the Back Door: Academic Racism and the Negro Scholar in Historical Perspective," *Daedalus* (Summer 1971): 678–720. Professor Winston's article is an incisive and well-documented analysis both of white academic racism and the formation of a school of Black scholars that counterpoised the white scholars.

15. *The Tragic Era* (Boston: Houghton Mifflin, 1929).

16. Ibid., p. 364.

17. Ibid.

18. Modern Library Edition (New York, 1945).

19. Ibid., p. 254.

20. Ibid., p. 255.

21. Appleton Century Co. (New York, 1936).

22. Ibid., p. 128.

23. As quoted in Winston, p. 686, from Albert B. Hart's *The Southern South* (New York: Appleton & Co., 1912).

24. As quoted, p. 687, in Winston, op. cit. The quotation is from "Social and Mental Traits of the American Negro," Howard W. Odum, in his *American Sociology: The Story of Sociology in the United States Through 1950* (New York: Longmans, Green, 1951).

25. Oliver Cromwell Cox, "Introduction" to Nathan Hare, *The Black Anglo-Saxons* (New York: The Macmillan Co., 1965), p. 28.

26. As quoted, ibid., Robert E. Park and Ernest W. Burgess, *Introduction to the Science of Sociology.*

27. Park, as quoted in Oliver Cromwell Cox, *Caste, Class, and Race* (New York: Monthly Review Press, 1959), p. 469, from Bertram W. Doyle, *The Etiquette of Race Relations in the South*, p. xx.

28. Allen Tate, as quoted in Addison Gayle, Jr., "Cultural Hegemony," *Amistad I* (New York: Vintage, February 1970).

29. *I'll Take My Stand,* by Twelve Southerners (New York: Harper & Row, 1930), p. 260.

30. Ibid., p. 174.

31. Allen Tate, "A View of the Whole South," *American Review II* (February 1934): 411–32.

32. Donald Davidson, "Still Rebels, Still Yankees," *American Review II* (November 1933).

33. As quoted in Addison Gayle, Jr., op. cit., p. 23.

34. McGraw-Hill (New York, 1950).

35. Ibid., p. 143.

36. Robert K. Carr, Donald H. Morrison, Maurer D. Bernstein, and Richard C. Snyder (New York: Rinehart & Co. Inc., 1951).

37. Robert K. Carr, et al. (New York: Holt, Rinehart and Winston, Inc., 1963), p. 63.

38. Ibid., p. 70.

39. Ibid., p. 314.

40. Ibid., p. 595.

41. Ibid., p. 853.

42. Alfred A. Knopf (New York, 1951).

43. For other examples see the 1952 edition of *Government by the People: The Dynamics of American National Government,* by James MacGregor Burns and Jack Walter Peltason (Englewood Cliffs, N.J.: Prentice-Hall, Inc., 1952); *Politics and Social Life,* by Nelson W. Polsby, Robert A. Dentler, and Paul A. Smith (Boston: Houghton Mifflin Co., 1963); a major text in political behavior, this work is a compendium of seventy articles on the subject. Two of the seventy articles deal with Black people and both, naturally, are written by whites. Also see Nick Aaron Ford, "The English Department and the Challenge of Racism," *Integrated Education* VII (July-August 1969): 24–30, where he notes that major college anthologies in English and American literature over the years have excluded works of Black authors.

44. Free Press (Glencoe, Ill., 1960).

45. James Q. Wilson, "Black and White Tragedy," *Encounter* XXIX (October 1967), p. 65.

46. Ibid., p. 66.

47. Ibid., p. 67.

48. Little, Brown (Boston, 1968, 1970).

49. Ibid., p. 62.

50. Ibid., p. 69.

51. Ibid., pp. 211–12.

52. Ibid., p. 85.

53. Ibid., p. 231.

54. *New York Times,* October 13, 1970. The publication day of *The Unheavenly City* was April 7, 1970.

55. MIT Press (Cambridge, Mass., 1963).

56. "America's Race Paradox," XXXI (October 1968): 9–18.

57. Ibid., p. 14.

58. W. E. B. Du Bois and Augustus Evanville Dill, "College-Bred Negro American," Atlantic University Publications (Arno Press and the *New York Times,* 1968), p. 46.

59. Richard L. Plautt, "Racial Integration in Public Higher Education in the North," *Journal of Negro Education* XXIII (Summer 1954).

60. "College-Bred Negro American," op. cit., pp. 23–24.

61. "Ivy League Negro," *Esquire* (August 1963): 54–57.

62. *No Day of Triumph* (New York: Harper & Row, 1942), p. 39.

63. "Soul in Suburbia," *Harper's Magazine* (January 1972), 24–31.

64. "Home Is Much Too Far to Go," *Black Review I* (New York: William Morrow Co., 1971), pp. 48–58. For an excellent sociological dissection of the feelings of Black students on four white upstate

New York campuses where the proportion of Blacks was below 2 per cent, see Charles V. Willie and Arline Sakuma McCord, *Black Students at White Colleges* (New York: Frederick A. Praeger, 1972).

65. *The Negro Caravan, op. cit.,* p. 397.

66. "College-Bred Negro American," op. cit., p. 40.

67. Plautt, op. cit., p. 313.

68. Redding, op. cit., see also Kelley, op. cit., passim.

69. Redding, op. cit., p. 39.

70. Kelley, op. cit., p. 56.

71. Woodson, op. cit., pp. 18, 34.

72. Jack Olsen, *The Black Athlete* (New York and Chicago: Time-Life Books, 1968), passim.

73. "The New Heaven and the New Earth," *Journal of Negro Education* XXVII (Spring 1958): 115–19.

CHAPTER 4

1. Nisbet, op. cit., p. 146.

2. *New York Times* (October 17, 1971).

3. Fred E. Crossland, *Minority Access to College,* a Ford Foundation Report (New York: Schocken Books, 1971), p. 34. Crossland, as many others, admits that data collection in colleges is in such a chaotic state that errors to the magnitude of 10 per cent may be present in these numbers (p. 9).

4. John Egerton, *State Universities and Black Americans* (Atlanta, Ga.: Southern Education Reporting Service, May 1969), p. 21.

5. Figures cited in Julian C. Stanley, "Predicting College Success of Educationally Disadvantaged Students," and drawn from CEEB studies in *Barriers to Higher Education* (New York: CEEB, 1971), p. 67.

6. *Equality of Educational Opportunity* (U.S. Department of Health, Education, and Welfare, Office of Education), Harold Howe, II, director of project.

7. Bernard D. Karpinos, "The Mental Test Qualification of American Youths for Military Service and Its Relationship to Educational Attainment," *Proceedings of the Social Statistics Section* (Washington, D.C.: American Statistical Association, 1966), pp. 92 ff.

8. For example, an undergraduate at Cornell in 1960 said: "You may think we're militant, but we may be seen by some people back in the community as Uncle Toms just because we went to a white university." *New York Times,* June 3, 1968.

9. *Cox Commission Report: Crisis at Columbia* (New York: Vintage, 1968), p. 16.

10. Chicago *Sun Times,* May 12, 1968.

11. Richard J. Margolis, "The Two Nations at Wesleyan," *New York Times Magazine*, January 18, 1970.

12. *New York Times*, June 3, 1968.

13. Ibid.

14. Margolis, op. cit.

15. Daril M. Rafky, "Wit and Racial Conflict," *Integrated Education* 10 (January–February 1972): 38–43.

16. G. Louis Heath, "An Inquiry into a University's 'Noble Savage' Program," *Integrated Education* 8 (July–August 1970): 4–9.

17. Mario D. Fantini and Gerald Weinstein, *The Disadvantaged* (New York: Harper & Row, 1968).

18. See James B. Conant, *The Education of American Teachers* (New York: McGraw-Hill, 1963).

19. As quoted, Fantini and Weinstein, op. cit., pp. 220–21.

20. Bertram Sandweiss, "The Teachers Adapt to the Custodial School," in August Kerber and Barbara Bommarito, *The Schools and the Urban Crisis* (New York: Holt, Rinehart and Winston, 1965), p. 220.

21. *Racial Isolation in the Public Schools*, U.S. Commission on Civil Rights (U.S. Government Printing Office, 1967).

CHAPTER 5

1. *New York Times*, April 23, 1970.

2. See his "Toward a 'Middle Way' in College Admissions," *Educational Record* 51 (Spring 1970): 106–110.

3. *The Campus and the Racial Crisis*, ed. by David C. Nichols and Olive Mills (Washington, D.C.: American Council on Education, 1970), pp. 29–30.

4. Ibid., p. 40.

5. Also see his and Irene Tinker's "Perspective on Black Studies," *Educational Record* (Winter 1971).

6. "Two Models of Open Enrollment," A. J. Jaffe and Walter Adams in *Universal Higher Education, Costs and Benefits* (Washington, D.C.: American Council on Education, 1971), pp. 143–69.

7. Julian C. Stanley, "Predicting College Success of Educationally Disadvantaged Students," using figures from *Barriers to Higher Education* (New York: CEEB, 1971), p. 66.

8. Ibid., p. 73.

9. *Black Education: Myths and Tragedies* (New York: David McKay, 1972).

10. Ibid., p. 45.

11. Ibid., p. 111.

12. Ibid., p. 135.

13. Ibid., p. 200.

14. Ibid., pp. 291–92.

15. Stanley, op. cit., pp. 67–68.

16. The study is *Negro Higher Education in the 1960s,* by A. J. Jaffe, Walter Adams, and Sandra G. Meyers (New York: Frederick A. Praeger, 1968). See Sowell, pp. 138–39.

17. Fred E. Crossland, *Minority Access to College,* A Ford Foundation Report (New York: Schocken Books, 1971), p. 59.

18. Ibid., p. 60.

19. Stanley, op. cit., pp. 59–60.

20. Sowell, op. cit., p. 177.

21. Agnew, op. cit., p. 107.

22. Ibid., p. 111.

23. Sowell, op. cit., p. 198.

24. Arthur R. Jensen, *Environment, Heredity, and Intelligence,* Reprint Series No. 2, compiled for the Harvard Educational Review, 1969.

25. Ibid., p. 28.

26. Ibid., p. 58.

27. Ibid., p. 59.

28. Ibid., p. 73.

29. Ibid., p. 82.

30. *The Open Door College,* Carnegie Commission on Higher Education (June 1970).

31. All examples are taken from writing samples of the Writing Center of the City College of New York.

32. *Chronicle of Higher Education* (April 5, 1971).

33. *Wall Street Journal* (March 17, 1970).

34. See Humphrey Doermann, "Lack of Money: A Barrier to Higher Education," in *Barriers to Higher Education,* pp. 130–46, for an extensive review of the financial needs of Black college youth.

CHAPTER 6

1. *Black Studies in the University,* ed. by Armistead L. Robinson, Craig C. Foster, and Donald H. Ogilvie (New York: Bantam, 1969).

2. Ibid., p. 26.

3. Ibid., p. 34.

4. Ibid., p. 180.

5. Ibid., p. 181. Bundy then went on to add that he felt all of these limitations could be overcome quickly.

6. Reprinted by permission in *New Perspectives on Black Studies,* ed. by John W. Blassingame (Urbana, Ill.: University of Illinois Press, 1971), pp. 104–15.

7. Ibid., p. 107.

8. Ibid., p. 108.

9. Ibid., p. 111.

10. See in Blassingame, ed., op. cit.; Kenneth Clark, "A Charade

of Power: Black Students at White Colleges," pp. 116–22, reprinted
from *The Antioch Review* 2 (Summer 1969); and W. Arthur Lewis,
"The Road to the Top Is Through Higher Education—Not Black
Studies," reprinted from the *New York Times Magazine*, May 11,
1969, pp. 133–48.

11. Lewis, op. cit., p. 141.

12. Harvard University, *Report of the Afro-American Studies Department* (September 21, 1970).

13. *New York Times* (December 27, 1970).

14. Frye Gaillard, "Vanderbilt Adjusts to Black Studies," *Race Relations Reporter* (November 1, 1971), p. 10.

15. Fred E. Crossland, "Graduate Education and Black Americans," Office of Special Projects, The Ford Foundation, November 26, 1968.

16. W. E. B. Du Bois, *Autobiography of W. E. B. Du Bois* (New York: International Publications, 1968) p. 198.

17. Position Paper; Malcolm X Liberation University (Greensboro, N.C.: n.d.), p. 2.

CHAPTER 7

1. April 11, 1964.

2. Commission on Admissions Report, October 7, 1969, p. 39.

3. Robert Birnbaum and Joseph Goldman, *The Graduates* (New York: Center for Social Research, CUNY, Office for Research in Higher Education, May 1971).

4. *New York Times*, May 29, 1969.

5. Ibid., May 27, 1969.

6. Ibid.

7. October 16, 1969.

8. *Hearing* (on open admissions) (October 22, 1969), p. 69.

9. Ibid.

10. Ibid., p. 188.

11. Ibid., p. 240.

12. Ibid., pp. 61–63.

13. *Open Admissions: Pros and Cons* (Washington, D.C.: Council for Basic Education, 1972).

14. Ibid., p. 23.

15. Ibid., p. 24.

16. Ibid., p. 20.

17. Ibid., p. 57.

18. Ibid., p. 54.

19. Ibid., p. 55.

20. Ibid., p. 59.

21. Ibid., p. 68.

22. Ibid., p. 34.

23. Ibid., p. 36.

CHAPTER 8

1. BLS Report No. 394—Current Population Reports, Series P-23, No. 38, *Special Studies: The Social and Economic Status of Negroes in the United States, 1970,* U.S. Department of Commerce; Bureau of Census; U.S. Department of Labor, Bureau of Labor Statistics. As the Census Bureau itself acknowledges, these figures may be off by as much as 5 to 10 per cent.

2. John Egerton, *The Black Public Colleges* (Race Relations Information Center, June 1971).

Index

0-595-31766-9